"From grade inflation to global calamities, Albert Mohler is a steady guide. From the psychological coddling of the American ego to the hollowing of the American conscience, Mohler is unremittingly clear-headed. From Nineveh to New Orleans, Mohler holds the mirror at a blazing forty-five-degree angle between heaven and earth. The burning light of divine wisdom illumines a hundred shadows of our human folly. And at the center of the blaze is the mighty cross of Jesus Christ defining the final meaning of everything. I thank God for Albert Mohler."

—JOHN PIPER, pastor for preaching, Bethlehem
Baptist Church, Minneapolis, MN

"Al Mohler is a unique gift to the church. His writing combines penetrating theological discernment and insightful cultural analysis with a passion to faithfully proclaim the gospel of Jesus Christ. I'm delighted that Al's wisdom is now available in this book."

—C. J. MAHANEY, Sovereign Grace Ministries

"We all know, as Dorothy said to Toto, that 'we are not in Kansas anymore.' But how to apply the deep truths of our Christian faith to a culture that seems to be transmogrifying before our very eyes, well, that's perhaps the most difficult question facing the church today. In this well-written book,

Al Mohler surveys the landscape and offers insight and wisdom that helps us do just this. A manifesto for responsible Christian engagement!"

—TIMOTHY GEORGE, founding dean of Beeson Divinity School of Samford University and senior editor of *Christianity Today*

"Thoughtful Christians seeking to engage the culture from a well-informed and thoroughly bibilical perspective will find an impressive resource in this work by R. Albert Mohler. *Culture Shift* is an outstanding contribution, which I heartily recommend."

—DAVID S. DOCKERY, president, Union University

"Dr. Albert Mohler brings his intellectual brilliance, moral wisdom, and theological insight together in a book that belongs on the shelf of anyone who is interested in both understanding the shifting sands of morality in our culture and how to deal with them. If you are in that category this is a must read."

—JAMES MERRITT, senior pastor of Cross Pointe Church, Duluth, GA, and host of Touching Lives media ministry

"Understanding our culture is a matter of Christian responsibility. *Culture Shift* helps us to do that and do it well."

—DANIEL L. AKIN, president, Southeastern Baptist Theological Seminary, Wake Forest, NC

CULTURE SHIFT

CULTURE SHIFT

The Battle for the Moral Heart of America

R. ALBERT MOHLER JR

MULTNOMAH
BOOKS

CULTURE SHIFT
PUBLISHED BY MULTNOMAH BOOKS
12265 Oracle Boulevard, Suite 200
Colorado Springs, Colorado 80921

All Scripture quotations, unless otherwise indicated, are taken from the New American Standard Bible®. © Copyright The Lockman Foundation 1960, 1962, 1963, 1968, 1971, 1972, 1973, 1975, 1977, 1995. Used by permission. (www.Lockman.org). Scripture quotations marked (ESV) are taken from The Holy Bible, English Standard Version, copyright © 2001 by Crossway Bibles, a division of Good News Publishers. Used by permission. All rights reserved. Scripture quotations marked (NIV) are taken from the Holy Bible, New International Version®. NIV®. Copyright © 1973, 1978, 1984 by International Bible Society. Used by permission of Zondervan Publishing House. All rights reserved.

ISBN 978-1-60142-381-8

Published in association with the literary agency of Wolgemuth & Associates Inc.

Published in the United States by WaterBrook Multnomah, an imprint of the Crown Publishing Group, a division of Random House Inc., New York.

MULTNOMAH and its mountain colophon are registered trademarks of Random House Inc.

The Library of Congress cataloged the hardcover edition as follows:
Mohler Jr., R. Albert, 1959–
    Culture shift / R. Albert Mohler.
      p. cm.
    Includes bibliographical references and index.
    ISBN 978-1-59052-974-4 (alk. paper)
  1. United States—Church history. 2. Christianity and culture—United States.
3. Christianity and politics—United States. I. Title.
    BR515.M56 2008
    261.0973—dc22

                                                    2007031614

Printed in the United States of America
2011—First Trade Paperback Edition

10 9 8 7 6 5 4 3 2 1

SPECIAL SALES
Most WaterBrook Multnomah books are available in special quantity discounts when purchased in bulk by corporations, organizations, and special-interest groups. Custom imprinting or excerpting can also be done to fit special needs. For information, please e-mail SpecialMarkets@WaterBrookPress.com or call 1-800-603-7051.

CONTENTS

Acknowledgments xiii

Preface xv

1 **Engaging the City of Man** 1
  Christian Faith and Politics

2 **Christian Morality and Public Law** 7
  Three Secular Arguments

3 **Christian Morality and Public Law** 15
  Three Secular Myths

4 **Christian Morality and Public Law** 23
  Five Theses

5 **The Culture of Offendedness** 29
  A Christian Challenge

6 **A Growing Cloud of Confusion** 37
  The Supreme Court on Religion

7 **All That Terror Teaches** 47
  Have We Learned Anything?

8 **Needed: An Exit Strategy from Public Schools** . . . 53
  The Crisis Christian Parents Face

9 **The God Gene** 61
  Bad Science Meets Bad Theology

10 **Are We Raising a Nation of Wimps?** 69
    A Coddled Generation Cannot Cope

11 **Hard America, Soft America** 77
    The Battle for America's Future

12 **The Post-Truth Era** 83
    Welcome to the Age of Dishonesty

13 **Is Abortion a Moral Issue?** 91
    A Fascinating Debate on the Left

14. **Who's Afraid of the Fetus?** 101
    How America's Abortion Debate Is Changing

15 **God and the Tsunami** 109
    Theology in the Headlines

16 **God and the Tsunami** 117
    A Christian Response

17 **Nineveh, New Orleans, and the City of Man** . . . 125
    An Eternal Perspective

18 **Hiroshima and the Burden of History** 133
    A Transforming Event

19 **The Content of Our Character** 143
    King's Dream and Ours

20 **The Challenge of Islam** 149
    A Christian Perspective

21 **The New Atheism**. 157
    Darwinism Makes Disbelief "Work"

22 **A Black Cat in a Dark Room** 163
    Are Theologians Really Saying Anything?

23 **The New American Family** 169
    Digitally Deluged

24 **Where Did I Come From?**. 175
    The New World of Reproductive Technology

25 **Redefining Retirement**. 183
    For the Good of the Kingdom

To Mary,
Who has added beyond measure to every dimension of my life,
and whose love and dedication inspires my every thought.

ACKNOWLEDGMENTS

I want to thank all those who have given such great assistance to me in this process. First, I thank my family—my wonderful wife, Mary, and our children, Katie and Christopher. They love and support a husband and dad who is preoccupied with these issues and brings them home for dinner. Their constant love and encouragement is a precious gift.

I also want to thank my research assistant, Greg Gilbert, and the faithful and helpful staff of my office at the Southern Baptist Theological Seminary and *The Albert Mohler Program*.

PREFACE

Aristotle once described our challenge as the problem of a fish in water. Knowing nothing but life in the water, the fish never even realizes it is wet. This describes the situation of many Christians in America—they do not even know that they are wet.

We are swimming in one of the most complex and challenging cultural contexts ever experienced by the Christian church. Every day brings a confrontation with cultural messages, controversies, and products. We are bombarded with advertisements, entertainments, and the chatter of the culture all around us. We are Aristotle's fish.

How are Christians to remain faithful as we live in this culture? How should we think about so many of the crucial moral questions of our day?

These questions are not merely academic. They will eventually touch every church and every Christian family. Our homes are constantly invaded by the culture all around us. Our children are targeted by advertisers and the marketplace of ideas. Entertainment has become a constant—symbolized by the satellite dish, the iPod, and the smart phone. There is no place to hide.

Moreover, the pace at which our culture is changing has accelerated over the past several decades. Transformations in the law, government, social morality, and education have accompanied the radical advances in technology and knowledge that mark our era. Like an earthquake that is caused when the tectonic plates on the earth's surface begin to shift, we are experiencing a seismic event in our culture.

How are Christians to think about these new cultural challenges? Some Christians prefer not to think seriously about these issues. This falls far short of an acceptable posture, however. Those who do not think seriously about how Christians should respond to these challenges will find that the dominant culture will simply pull them into its vortex. They will simply fail to live and think as Christians.

Others think they can somehow evade the culture. In reality, this is impossible. We may try to remove ourselves and our children from the culture, but the culture will find us. We use language, wear clothing, and engage as consumers in a world of continuous cultural invasion. The culture is a vast network of institutions, laws, customs, and language that is a constant part of our lives, like it or not.

Still others try to embrace the culture without reservation. This doesn't work either. An honest evaluation reveals that many of the most cherished assumptions of our culture are in direct conflict with the teachings of Christ. We cannot accept the idea that we are what we consume and possess. We cannot accept the denial of human dignity that underlies this culture's acceptance of the destruction of human life in the womb and in the laboratory. We cannot buy in to the cherished myth of autonomous individualism, and we cannot compromise with a worldview based on the assumption that truth is relative or socially constructed.

At the same time, we remember that our Lord gave His church an evangelistic commission—to be witnesses of the gospel. Every single person we will try to reach with the gospel is embedded in some culture. Understanding the culture thus becomes a matter of evangelistic urgency.

Jesus was confronted one day by a lawyer who asked Him: "Teacher, which is the great commandment in the Law?" Jesus answered: "You shall love the Lord your God with all your heart and with all your soul and with all your mind. This is the great and first commandment. And a second is like it: You shall love your neighbor as yourself. On these two commandments depend all the Law and the Prophets" (Matthew 22:36–40, ESV).

Jesus told that lawyer—and His own disciples—that our first priority is to love God with heart and soul and mind. Our second priority is to love our neighbor as ourselves. As the Lord said: "On these two commandments depend all the Law and the Prophets."

In other words, the Christian life is summarized in these two commands. We must first understand our culture and its challenges because we are to be faithful followers of Christ and faithful witnesses to the gospel. We are called to faithfulness, and faithfulness requires that we be ready to think as Christians when confronted with the crucial issues of the day. This is all rooted in our love of God.

But Jesus also commanded love of neighbor, and Christians must be driven by love of neighbor as we confront the issues of our day. We care for the well-being of our neighbors, and we want to see them come to faith in Christ. We care about marriage, sexuality, children, the dignity of human life, and a host of related issues because we love God first, and this leads directly to love of our neighbor—and our neighborhood.

In the end, the culture and its challenges will pass away. But our Lord has left us here for a reason—as His people, we are to be salt and light in a dying world.

My hope is that these essays will assist you as you seek to be faithful to Christ as a concerned and intelligent Christian.

1

ENGAGING THE CITY OF MAN

Christian Faith and Politics

O ver the last twenty years, evangelical Christians have been politically mobilized in an outpouring of moral concern and political engagement unprecedented since the crusade against slavery in the nineteenth century. Is this a good development? Given the issues now confronting our nation, the issue of political involvement emerges anew with urgency. To what extent should Christians be involved in the political process?

This question has troubled the Christian conscience for centuries. The emergence of the modern evangelical movement in the post–World War II era brought a renewed concern for engagement with the culture and the political process. The late Carl F. H. Henry addressed evangelicals with a manifesto for Christian engagement in his landmark book *The Uneasy Conscience of Modern Fundamentalism.*[1] As Dr. Henry eloquently argued, disengagement from the critical issues of the day is not an option.

An evangelical theology for political participation must be grounded in the larger context of cultural engagement. As the Christian worldview makes clear, our ultimate concern must be the glory of God. When Scripture instructs us to love God and then to love our neighbor as ourselves, it thereby gives us a clear mandate for the right kind of cultural engagement.

We love our neighbor because we first love God. In His sovereignty, our Creator has put us within this cultural context in order that we may display His glory by preaching the gospel, confronting persons with God's truth, and serving as agents of salt and light in a dark and fallen world. In other words, love of God leads us to love our neighbor, and love of neighbor requires our participation in the culture and in the political process.

Writing as the Roman Empire fell, Augustine, the great bishop and theologian of the early church, made this case in his monumental work *The City of God.*[2] As Augustine ex-

---

1. Carl F. H. Henry, *The Uneasy Conscience of American Fundamentalism* (Grand Rapids: Eerdmans, 2003). Originally published in 1947.

2. Augustine, *The City of God Against the Pagans*, Cambridge Texts in the History of Political Thought (Cambridge: Cambridge University Press, 1998).

plained, humanity is confronted by two cities—the City of God and the City of Man. The City of God is eternal and takes as its sole concern the greater glory of God. In the City of God, all things are ruled by God's Word, and the perfect rule of God is the passion of all its citizens.

In the City of Man, however, the reality is very different. This city is filled with mixed passions, mixed allegiances, and compromised principles. Unlike the City of God, whose citizens are marked by unconditional obedience to the commands of God, citizens of the City of Man demonstrate deadly patterns of disobedience, even as they celebrate, claim their moral autonomy, and then revolt against the Creator.

Of course, we know that the City of God is eternal, even as the City of Man is passing. But this does not mean that the City of Man is ultimately unimportant, and it does not allow the church to forfeit its responsibility to love its citizens. Love of neighbor—grounded in our love for God—requires us to work for good in the City of Man, even as we set as our first priority the preaching of the gospel—the only means of bringing citizens of the City of Man into citizenship in the City of God.

Because of this, Christians bear important responsibilities in both cities. Even as we know that our ultimate citizenship is in heaven, and even as we set our sights on the glory of the City of God, we must work for good, justice, and righteousness in the City of Man. We do so, not merely because we are commanded to love its citizens, but because we know that they are loved by the very God we serve.

From generation to generation, Christians often swing between two extremes, either ignoring the City of Man or considering it to be our main concern. A biblical balance establishes the fact that the City of Man is indeed passing and chastens us from believing that the City of Man and its realities can ever be of ultimate importance. Yet we also know that each of us is by God's own design a citizen, however temporarily, of the City of Man. When Jesus instructed that we are to love our neighbor as ourselves, He pointed His followers to the City of Man and gave us a clear assignment. The only alternatives that remain are obedience and disobedience to this call.

Love of neighbor for the sake of loving God is a profound political philosophy that strikes a balance between the disobedience of political disengagement and the idolatry of politics as our main priority. As evangelical Christians, we must engage in political action, not because we believe the conceit that politics is ultimate, but because we must obey our Redeemer when He commands us to love our neighbor. On the other hand, we are concerned for the culture, not because we believe that the culture is ultimate, but because we know that our neighbors must hear the gospel, even as we hope and strive for their good, peace, security, and well-being.

The kingdom of God is never up for a vote in any election, and there are no polling places in the City of God. Nevertheless, it is by God's sovereignty that we are now confronted with these times, our current crucial issues of debate, and the decisions that are made in the political process. This is no time for silence or for shirking our responsibilities as Christian citizens. Ominous signs of moral collapse and cultural decay now appear on our contemporary horizon. A society ready to put the institution of marriage up for demolition and transformation is a society losing its most basic moral sense. A culture ready to treat human embryos as material for medical experimentation is a society turning its back on human dignity and the sacredness of human life.

Trouble in the City of Man is a call to action for the citizens of the City of God, and that call to action must involve political involvement as well. Christians may well be the last people who know the difference between the eternal and the temporal, the ultimate and the urgent. God's truth is eternal, and Christian convictions must be commitments of permanence. Political alliances and arrangements are, by definition, temporary and conditional. This is no time for America's Christians to confuse the City of Man with the City of God. At the same time, we can never be counted faithful in the City of God if we neglect our duty in the City of Man.

2

CHRISTIAN MORALITY AND PUBLIC LAW

Three Secular Arguments

How should Christian morality and public law relate to each other? This is a quintessentially modern question. In other eras of Christian history, or even the history of Western civilization, to ask how Christian morality and public law should be related would have been to ask an incomprehensible question. Most people would have understood morality and law to be one and the same thing, or they would have seen public law merely as a tangible structure and definition of Christian morality. Throughout most of Christian history and the history of Western nations, law and morality were understood as being on parallel tracks, indispensable to each other. Public laws were simply the codification of a moral worldview.

Now we live in a day in which that understanding is completely changed. With the advent of modernity, and now the postmodern age, the view that public law is or ought to be predicated on Christian morals is no longer taken for granted. Not only is that idea questioned, but it is even rejected out of hand. Many in Western societies are now absolutely convinced that there should in fact be *no* relationship whatsoever between Christian morality and public law. For these, it is just as axiomatic that public law should be essentially secular as it once was for others that it must be essentially Christian.

That ideology, properly known as secularism, suggests that there is an *oughtness* to the secularization of the public space, that the culture *ought* to be established on purely secular terms without any reference at all to a theistic reality or a theistic accountability. At the popular level, secularism as an ideology has never been well accepted in America. It has, however, become rather pervasive at the level of the cultural and intellectual elite, a necessary component in the elite class's struggle to advance its own norms and values system. The persons who sit on federal judiciaries and hold positions of symbolic importance and cultural influence tend to hold this secular worldview, at least with a tenacity and in percentages far beyond that of the general public.

And what do these people say about the intersection of Christian morality and public law? For the secularist who believes that America's public space should be essentially and irreducibly secular, that question is easy. There should be *no* relationship at all. Public law should not be dependent on Christian morality, and Christian morality should have no influence on public law. Indeed, laws should never be determined or even shaped by any institution or idea that is self-consciously tied to Christian morality or even unselfconsciously derivative of Christian morality.

Let me offer three examples of those who hold to such a position. First is Robert Reich, the former secretary of labor in the Clinton administration. A former faculty member at Harvard University, Reich is a thoughtful person to whom we are indebted for many insightful writings. In 2004 Reich wrote a new book titled *Reason: Why Liberals Will Win the Battle for America*.[1] In this book he identifies the opposition—those who hold the worldview that should be countered and defeated—as the "Radcons," a short compound for "radical conservatives." The individual who stands as a symbol of the Radcons is William Bennett, former secretary of education and drug czar. The Radcons believe that morality must be based upon some larger worldview. Christianity should be recognized and respected as the worldview that gave shape to Western civilization, they argue.

So what should be done with the Radcons? Reich says this: "It's perfectly fine for Radcons to declare strong personal

---

1. Robert Reich, *Reason: Why Liberals Will Win the Battle for America* (New York: Knopf, 2004).

convictions about sex and marriage—convictions often based on sincere religious beliefs. But it is quite another thing to insist that everyone else must share the same convictions. As I've said, the liberal tradition has wisely drawn a sharp boundary between religion and government. We've got to stop the Radcons before they impose their narrow-minded agenda any further."

He then parodies the Radcon understanding of descent down a slippery moral slope: "Here is a real slippery slope that *does* concern me. Once we allow Radcons or anyone else to decide how we should conduct our private sex lives, where would it end? If we accept the idea that one religion's view about proper morality should be the law of the land, how do we decide whose religious views should prevail?"[2] Robert Reich is one example of a person who believes Christian morality should have no voice in the public square.

A second example is Robert Audi, professor of philosophy at the University of Notre Dame and the nation's most noted advocate of a pure secular space in terms of public policy. Audi offers three principles for what he calls "civic virtue in a liberal democracy." The first of these he calls the principle of *secular rationale*. This principle, Audi writes, says that one "has as a *prima facie* obligation not to advocate or support any law or public policy that restricts human conduct, unless one has and is willing to offer, adequate sec-

---

2. Reich, *Reason,* 61–62.

ular reason for its advocacy or support."[3] Secular reasons, that is, must be the sole point of advocacy.

"There must be," he says, "a secular rationale that is understood to be a secular reason." The only acceptable reason is a purely secular one, that is, "roughly one whose normative force, that is, its status as a prima facie justificatory element, does not evidentially depend on the existence of God (or on denying it) or on theological considerations, or on the pronouncements of a person or institution *qua* religious authority."[4] In other words, any reason given for adopting any public policy must be irreducibly secular, manifestly secular, entirely secular—that is, with no reference whatsoever to the existence or nonexistence of any God.

Second, Audi suggests a principle of *secular motivation*. He explains:

> One has a prima facie obligation to abstain from advocacy or support of a law or public policy that restricts human conduct, unless…one is sufficiently motivated by a (normatively) adequate secular reason. Sufficiency of motivation here implies that some set of secular reasons is motivationally sufficient, roughly in the sense that (a) this set of reasons

---

3. Robert Audi, *Religious Commitment and Secular Reason* (Cambridge: Cambridge University Press, 2000), 86.
4. Audi, *Religious Commitment and Secular Reason,* 89.

explains one's action and (b) one would act on it even if, other things remaining equal, one's other reasons were eliminated.[5]

In other words, any religious motivation is ruled out-of-bounds. Not only must a person advocating a public-policy position have a purely secular rationale, but his advocacy must be secularly motivated as well. It is not enough to offer secular arguments for a position if one's real reason for holding it is a belief in God.

Finally, Audi offers the principle of *ecclesiastical political neutrality*. He says, "In a free and democratic society, churches committed to being institutional citizens in such a society have a prima facie obligation to abstain from supporting candidates for public office or pressing for laws or public policies that restrict human conduct."[6] In other words, churches may do whatever churches wish to do, so long as they do not endorse political candidates (a restriction with which most of us would be quite satisfied) or "press for laws or public policies that restrict human conduct." That is more troubling, for most of us would want to be free to advocate laws that restrict human conduct in some ways.

A final example is law professor Kathleen Sullivan. Following the same logic, she says, "The correct baseline theory

---

5. Audi, *Religious Commitment and Secular Reason*, 96.
6. Audi, *Religious Commitment and Secular Reason*, 42.

is not unfettered religious liberty, but rather religious liberty insofar as it is consistent with the establishment of the secular, moral order."[7] That is a fascinating statement, one which amounts to a redefinition of religious liberty. The baseline, she says, is not unfettered religious liberty; those God-believers should be granted religious liberty only so long as their liberty does not interfere with the establishment of a secular moral order.

I bring these three witnesses because I believe they are being honest. Reich, Audi, and Sullivan call for a public space that is purely and completely secular. Not only must the shape and content of the arguments in the public square be secular, but the very motivation for making an argument at all must be entirely secular—as Audi would have it, without reference to whether or not there is even a God who exists. Any argument based on any premise which might be considered "religious" is categorically excluded. The honesty of these positions is helpful, for it sets the issues squarely and thus demonstrates immediately the implausibility of such proposals.

---

7. Kathleen M. Sullivan, "Religion and Liberal Democracy," *The University of Chicago Law Review,* vol. 59, no. 1 (Winter 1992).

3

CHRISTIAN MORALITY AND PUBLIC LAW

Three Secular Myths

Secularism rests on three myths. The first is *the myth of the secular state.* Secularism is not a positive construct. By its very nature, something is secular only when it *denies* the existence of God. Here is where Robert Audi's logic begins to break down. One cannot be genuinely secular and be indifferent to the existence of God, because if God did exist, that would bring immediate demands upon society—obligations and prohibitions that society would not be able simply to ignore without admitting that it is only *tacitly* or *operationally* secular. A truly secular state must altogether deny the existence of God. In other words, this is a call for an absolutely secular state—the existence of which is a myth. Why? Because states must deal with fundamental questions. They must deal with questions concerning life and death, questions about human identity, ultimate questions about existence and meaning in the universe. But the moment a state begins to deal with those fundamental questions, it ceases to be secular, especially the way Audi defines it, even at the motivational level. When states begin to effect laws and codify some morality, there is no way it can remain purely secular, because any question that addresses itself to the meaning of life and death, for example, must be considered in terms much larger than secular theory will allow. There is no truly secular state.

Second is *the myth of a secular argument*. No argument is truly irreducibly secular, for anyone who wants to make an argument about anything beyond procedure will have to deal with questions of meaning, morality, and value—questions that are larger than any individual human frame of reference. On issues like these, there are no arguments that are genuinely secular. As a matter of fact, listen carefully to those who most seek to advocate purely secular arguments. On questions of meaning and morality, their arguments are themselves just as essentially religious as the "religious" arguments they reject. They may believe their claims are not religious, but they end up being religious precisely because they are *anti*religious. Moreover, they attempt to set up their own version of God—their own idea of what is the ultimate good—in order to determine value.

Third is *the myth of secular motivation*. Motivation is an

inherently complex issue, because none of us is fully aware of our own motivation. This is the problem with the circular reasoning of Audi's principle of secular motivation. He expects people to disregard their beliefs about God in thinking about public policy and decide what they would believe about a certain issue if they did not already believe in God. But a human being can never know what he would believe if he were not motivated by what centrally motivates him. How can a person know that he would continue to advocate the same position if he no longer believed in God, or if belief in God were simply bracketed from the equation? Audi's position is simply unrealistic. No human being will ever know himself so well that he can separate himself from his own motivations, even one who allows himself the conceit of believing he is driven by a purely secular motivation. Furthermore, to move the focus of the national conversation from the objective content of an argument to its subjective motivation is to be no longer engaged in public-policy discussions, but rather in some kind of communal therapy session.

There is no genuinely secular state, no secular argument, and no secular motivation, even among those who consider themselves secular. There is no neutrality. On questions as ultimate as the existence or nonexistence of God, or the binding or nonbinding character of His dictates and commands, or the objectivity or subjectivity of morality, or the absoluteness or nonabsoluteness of truth, there are no mediating positions. There is no neutrality.

Insofar as the law deals with what is most important, it must deal with ultimate issues like these. The law certainly deals with some issues of mere procedure and with policies that are not inherently freighted with moral importance. Yet on these issues, we do not have intense public controversies. America is not now in danger of being divided in two over parking policies in the nation's capital, but over the institution of marriage. Passions are not running high over how certain procedures in the tax code could be rewritten, but on questions of normative sexuality. Heated debate over the federal budget may come and go, but the vital concern of whether a human embryo is recognized as bearing the dignity of life—and is thus deserving of protection—is an ultimate issue.

To argue over issues like these is to argue at a level far above a secular plane. It is to argue at the level of moral ultimacy—some from one perspective, some from another, but none from a genuinely secular perspective. Therefore, if we accept the argument that Christian moral arguments are forbidden entry into the public space, we have decided not only to violate the clear intention of our Constitution's framers, not only to reject the inherited civilization that has brought us to this point, not only to redefine what it means to be a liberal democracy, but we have actually privileged one form of religious discourse over another. That is, we have privileged *irreligious* religious discourse over self-consciously religious discourse.

Furthermore, how can society deal with ultimate issues if the only people who are genuinely allowed into the discussion are those who believe there is nothing more ultimate than our own existence, our own communal negotiation of moral questions? If ever we reach such a point, we will have become a civilization not even remotely like the one established by our Founders.

In every one of Robert Audi's principles, his precise concern is with laws that restrict human conduct. That is the heart of the issue. There is a libertarian philosophy behind this, a basic idea of the liberty of human conduct. Audi's suggestion is that any limitation on human conduct must be justified. This is the "justificatory principle" now discussed in law schools, which states that any restriction on human conduct must be socially mandated by the political process on purely secular grounds. But here again, there is a serious problem. Where can we find an adequate rationale for restricting human conduct on purely secular grounds?

Most people would agree that murder, for example, is inherently wrong. But why? Once the issue is pressed hard enough, the purely secular theorist has very little ground for argumentation. The question "Why?" eventually presses the secular argument back to its irreducibly and essentially *un*secular form. Why is murder wrong? Some might try to fashion an answer to this question on the grounds of pragmatism. William James, John Dewey, Stanley Fish, Richard Rorty, and others have argued that all issues of ultimacy must be adjudicated on pragmatic grounds. However, the problem is that human life, in terms of its inherent dignity, is very difficult to define in purely pragmatic terms.

For instance, when does human life begin? As Christians, we have a principled, axiomatic answer to that question. But how does a putatively secular theorist fashion an answer to that question? His first instinct, of course, will be to let science step in and adjudicate the issue. But science cannot answer that question, because in order to say when human life begins, there must be some definition of what human life *is,* and that definition is precisely what science cannot offer. Because of that, there is no consensus among secularists about the definition of human life. There is an entire spectrum among them about what human life should be, how it should be defined, when it begins, and when it is worthy of protection. There are secularists who hold that life begins at conception, and there are other secularists, like Peter Singer, who would argue that even infanticide should not be considered immoral. After all, a woman's right to choose is inviolable, and life, Singer says, is not worthy of protection until the human being has attained the ability to relate and use language.[1]

Singer's conclusions may be distasteful to the secular aesthetic—at least for now—but according to a purely secu-

---

1. See, for example, Peter Singer, *Practical Ethics* (Cambridge: Cambridge University Press, 1993), 83–109, 182.

lar rationale, can we really say he is *wrong*? He may be embarrassing in a political sense, but according to a purely secular moral evaluation, he cannot be said to be *wrong*. This inevitable moral fog is the fatal problem faced by those who try to approach ultimate questions with a purely secular worldview.

4

CHRISTIAN MORALITY AND PUBLIC LAW

Five Theses

Even though the law must deal with ultimate issues, the argument is still being made that Christian morality ought to be shut out of the public discourse. As Christians, we must face the fact that we enter a public square that many expect to be purely secular. So what should we do? I offer five theses for understanding the relationship of Christian morality to public law.

First, a liberal democracy must allow all participants in the debate to speak and argue from whatever worldviews or convictions they possess. A liberal democracy should say yes to the entry of all citizens into the public conversation. Those citizens will come from many different backgrounds, and they will represent many different worldviews, some more religious and some less, some more secular and some less, some more Christian and some less. But all should be allowed equal access to the conversation. This is a principle that lies at the very heart of a deliberative democracy. Each citizen must be allowed to speak from his deepest convictions and to identify those convictions without fear of prejudice or of being eliminated from the public debate.

Second, citizens participating in public debate over law and public policy should declare the convictional basis for their arguments. This is where intellectual honesty enters the national conversation. When I debate these issues in the public square, I try to find some way to make clear that I am speaking as a convictional Christian and that I come to my conclusions by following a certain line of argument that begins at A and ends at B. It is not always possible to articulate such a moral argument comprehensively, but one should at least be honest about the basis for the argument and, insofar as one knows one's self, about its motivation as well.

Third, a liberal democracy must accept limits on secular discourse even as it recognizes limits on religious discourse. Of course there are limits on religious discourse. We cannot, for example, take the church covenant of any particular church and make it municipal or national law. The First Amendment to the Constitution disallows the government from establishing a religion. We cannot codify something immediately into law simply because some authority or another says it; there is a deliberative, democratic process in this nation, and there are limits upon the imposition of a religious worldview. But even as we all accept that there are limits upon religious discourse in a liberal, deliberative democracy, we must also recognize that there are limits upon secular discourse. Most importantly, secular discourse does not have the right to eliminate Christian discourse.

Fourth, a liberal democracy must acknowledge the commingling of religious and secular arguments, religious and secular motivations, and religious and secular outcomes. This commingling takes place because we as Christians will argue from a normative moral basis and about moral content, but we will also make arguments about social effects, about the likely outcome of making one moral decision over against another. Even as we base our policy arguments in the moral norms of God's Word, there are also political and social implications to be considered and included in the discussion.

Fifth, a liberal democracy must acknowledge and respect the rights of all citizens, including its self-consciously religious citizens. One would think such a statement would be unnecessary, since the First Amendment to the Constitution specifically protects religious expression. But as Robert Audi and Kathleen Sullivan understand it, that amendment only protects religious expression insofar as it does not interfere with a purely secular political state. In other words, religious people may talk among themselves about how they would structure society, but they are not free to air those ideas outside the walls of their churches. Christians and their religious, moral arguments ought to be excluded from the national conversation. That idea, however, cannot possibly be reconciled with the founding vision of America or with the language of the Constitution or with how human beings actually think, act, and speak.

Speaking from Christian conviction, I would finally suggest for our consideration two principles that come directly from the Word of God and from the command of Jesus. In the greatest commandment, we are told to love the Lord our God with all our heart, all our soul, and all our mind. The second is like it: we are to love our neighbor as ourselves. A Christian's motivation for entering the public square and advocating public policy is love of neighbor. Our concern in political, moral, social, and cultural engagement is not to impose Christianity—as if the mere imposition of a Christian moral code would be sufficient. Rather, our concern is love for our neighbor. We are motivated by love for other human beings, believing that health and welfare and happiness and commonweal are dependent on society's being ordered in such a way that the Creator's intentions for human relationships are honored and upheld—and that will inevitably require restrictions on human conduct. Only when the Creator's intentions for human society are upheld will His desire for human happiness also be realized among us.

As Christians, we understand the law of the harvest—as we sow, so shall we reap—and thus we must make arguments about action and consequence that deal, not only with demographic and economic and cultural realities, but with issues far more important than any considered in the secular world. Love of neighbor means we are compelled out of concern for our fellow citizens to see the law and public policy rightly ordered in such a way that maximum human happiness will be achieved.

5

THE CULTURE OF OFFENDEDNESS

A Christian Challenge

A new and unprecedented right is now the central focus of legal, procedural, and cultural concern in many corridors—a supposed right not to be offended. The cultural momentum behind this purported right is growing fast, and the logic of this movement has taken hold in many universities, legal circles, and interest groups.

The larger world received a rude introduction to the logic of offendedness when riots broke out in many European cities in 2006, after a Danish newspaper published cartoons that reportedly mocked the prophet Muhammad. The logic of the riots was that Muslims deserved never to be offended by any insult, real or perceived, directed to their belief system. Unthinking Christians may fall into the same pattern of claiming offendedness whenever we face opposition to our faith or criticism of our beliefs. The risk of being offended is simply part of what it means to live in a diverse culture that honors and celebrates free speech. A right to free speech means a right to offend; otherwise the right would need no protection.

These days, it is the secularists who seem to be most intent on pushing a proposed right never to be offended by confrontation with the Christian gospel, Christian witness, or Christian speech and symbolism. This motivation lies behind the incessant effort to remove all symbols, representations, references, and images related to Christianity from the public square. The very existence of a large cross, placed on government property as a memorial outside San Diego, California, has been a major issue in the courts for two decades. Those pressing for the removal of the cross claim that they are offended by the fact that they are forced to see this Christian symbol from time to time.

We should note carefully that this notion of offendedness is highly emotive in character. In other words, those who now claim to be offended are generally speaking of an emotional state that has resulted from some real or perceived insult to their belief system or from contact with someone else's belief system. In this sense, being offended does not necessarily involve any real harm but points instead to the fact that the mere presence of such an argument, image, or symbol evokes an emotional response of offendedness.

The distinguished Christian philosopher Paul Helm addresses this issue in an article published in the Summer 2006 edition of the *Salisbury Review*, published in Great Britain. Professor Helm argues, "Historically, being offended has been a very serious matter. To be offended is to be caused to stumble so as to fall, to fail, to apostasize, to be brought down, to be crushed." As evidence for this claim, Professor Helm points to the language of the King James Bible in which Jesus says to his disciples: "And if thy right eye offend thee, pluck it out, and cast it from thee: for it is profitable for thee that one of thy members should perish, and not that thy whole body should be cast into hell" (Matthew 5:29). Likewise, Jesus also speaks a warning against those who would "offend" the "little ones" (Matthew 18:6).

Today, desperate straits are no longer required in order for an individual or group to claim the emotional status of offendedness. All that is required is often the vaguest notion of emotional distaste at what another has said, done, proposed, or presented. This shift in the meaning of the word and in its cultural usage is subtle but extremely significant. It also leads to inevitable conflict.

"People have always been upset by insensitivity and negligence, but the profile of offendedness, understood in this modern sense, is being immeasurably heightened," suggests Professor Helm. Now, "the right never to be offended" is not only accepted as legitimate, but is actually promoted by the media, by government, and by activist groups.

The very idea of civil society assumes the very real possibility that individuals may at any time be offended by another member of the community. Civilization thrives when individuals and groups seek to minimize unnecessary offendedness, while recognizing that some degree of real or perceived offendedness is the cost the society must pay for the right to enjoy the free exchange of ideas and the freedom to speak one's mind.

Professor Helm is surely right when he argues that the "social value" of offendedness is now increasing. All that is necessary for a claim to be taken seriously is for the claim to be offered. After all, if the essence of the offendedness is an emotional state or response, how can any individual deny that a claimant has been genuinely offended? Professor Helm is right to worry that this will lead to the fracturing of society.

> We all hear things we don't like said about people
> and causes that we are fond of but in the changed
> social atmosphere we are being encouraged to give
> public notice if such language offends us. I am now
> being repeatedly told that I am entitled not to be
> offended. So—from now on—not offended is what
> I intend to be. Does this heightening of sensitivity
> make for social cohesion? Does not such cohesion
> depend rather on enduring what we don't like, and
> doing so in an adult way? Does not the glue of civic

peace rest on such intangibles as the ability to laugh at oneself, to take a joke about even the deepest things? And is it not a measure of the strength of a person's religion that they tolerate the unpleasant conversation of others? Isn't playing the offendedness card going to result in an enfeebling of the culture, the development of oversensitive and precious members of the "caring society"? Whatever happened to toleration?[1]

Given our mandate to share the gospel and to speak openly and publicly about Jesus Christ and the Christian faith, Christians must understand a particular responsibility to protect free speech and to resist this culture of offendedness that threatens to shut down all public discourse. Of course, the right for Christians to speak publicly about Jesus Christ necessarily means that adherents of other belief systems will be equally free to present their truth claims in an equally public manner. This is simply the cost of religious liberty.

An interesting witness to this point is Salman Rushdie, the novelist who was once put under a Muslim sentence of death because he had insulted Muslim sensibilities in his novel *The Satanic Verses*. Mr. Rushdie presents an argument that Christians must take seriously.

---

1. Paul Helm, "Offendedness," *Salisbury Review*, June 2006, 16–18.

The idea that any kind of free society can be constructed in which people will never be offended or insulted is absurd. So too is the notion that people should have the right to call on the law to defend them against being offended or insulted. A fundamental decision needs to be made: do we want to live in a free society or not? Democracy is not a tea party where people sit around making polite conversation. In democracies people get extremely upset with each other. They argue vehemently against each other's positions.

Rushdie continues:

People have the fundamental right to take an argument to the point where somebody is offended by what they say. It is no trick to support the free speech of somebody you agree with or to whose opinion you are indifferent. The defense of free speech begins at the point where people say something you can't stand. If you can't defend their right to say it, then you don't believe in free speech. You only believe in free speech as long as it doesn't get up your nose.[2]

---

2. Both quotes are from Salman Rushdie, "Defend the Right to Be Offended," openDemocracy, February 7, 2005, www.opendemocracy .net/faith-europe_islam/article_2331.jsp.

As the apostle Paul made clear in writing to the Corinthians, the preaching of the gospel has always been considered offensive by those who reject it. When Paul spoke of the Cross as "foolishness" and a "stumbling block" (1 Corinthians 1:23, NIV), he was pointing to this very reality—a reality that would lead to his own stoning, flogging, imprisonment, and execution.

At the same time, Paul did not want to offend persons on the basis of anything *other* than the cross of Christ and the essence of the Christian gospel. For this reason, he would write to the Corinthians about becoming "all things to all people, that by all means I might save some" (1 Corinthians 9:22, ESV).

Without doubt, many Christians manage to be offensive for reasons other than the offense of the gospel. This is to our shame and to the injury of our gospel witness. Nevertheless, there is no way for a faithful Christian to avoid offending those who are offended by Jesus Christ and His cross. The truth claims of Christianity, by their very particularity and exclusivity, are inherently offensive to those who would demand some other gospel.

Christians must not only contend for the preservation and protection of free speech—essential for the cause of the gospel—we must also make certain that we do not fall into the trap of claiming offendedness for ourselves. We must not claim a right not to be offended, even as we must insist that there is no such right and that the social construction of such a right will mean the death of individual liberty, free speech, and the free exchange of ideas.

Once we begin playing the game of offendedness, there is no end to the matter. There simply is no right *not* to be offended, and we should be offended by the very notion that such a right could exist.

6

A GROWING CLOUD
OF CONFUSION

The Supreme Court
on Religion

Over the past half century, the U.S. Supreme Court has accomplished a feat America's Founders would surely have found to be inconceivable. They have created a perverse cloud of confusion over the question of religious liberty and the place of religious language and symbols in the public square.

Indeed, the confusion is now so pervasive that a consistent understanding of the Court's directives is practically impossible. In just a few short decades, the Court has decided that organized prayer must be removed from public-school classrooms, that religious symbolism must be removed from official seals and emblems, and that all references to a deity must be reduced to a merely ceremonial meaning if they are to be allowed at all. On the other hand, the federal courts have allowed for the military to pay chaplains, for the words "under God" to remain in the Pledge of Allegiance, and for both houses of Congress to employ chaplains and to begin each session with prayer.

The Court's decisions amount to a form of judicial sophistry. Take, for example, the question of nativity displays on public land. The Court allows that such displays *may* be allowable, but only if the Christmas scene is surrounded by the commercial paraphernalia of the season. In other words, the Christ child is allowed only insofar as Rudolph the Red-Nosed Reindeer, Santa Claus, and Frosty the Snowman are also present. But in 2005 the nation's High Court pushed its jurisprudence on these questions into even greater depths of confusion. This time, the issue was the public posting of the Ten Commandments.

Dealing with two separate cases, one from Kentucky and one from Texas, the Supreme Court came to two different conclusions. In two 5–4 decisions, with Justice Stephen Breyer casting the decisive fifth vote in both cases, the Court decided that a Kentucky display of the Ten Commandments was unconstitutional, even as it allowed a display of the same text on the grounds of the Texas capitol.[1] In other

---

1. *Van Orden v. Perry,* 545 U.S. 677 (2005) and *McCreary County v. American Civil Liberties Union of Kentucky,* 545 U.S. 844 (2005).

words, a majority of one vote found that the display of the Ten Commandments in McCreary County, Kentucky, violated the Constitution, while the display of the Decalogue in Texas was permissible. Confused?

Writing in the October 2005 issue of *American Spectator*, Professor Stephen B. Presser of Northwestern University's School of Law argues that "for sheer incoherence nothing beats the Court's 'establishment clause' jurisprudence."[2] The First Amendment famously includes two different clauses concerning religion. The positive clause assures that citizens are guaranteed the free exercise of religion. The second, known most commonly as the establishment clause, reads: "Congress shall make no law respecting an establishment of religion." That's all.

How did the Court transform itself into the source of such confusion? Presser, who holds the Raoul Berger Chair in Legal History at Northwestern, explains that the federal courts should have prevented this confusion by avoiding the cases altogether. "One might have thought, indeed, that because the establishment clause *only prohibits acts of Congress,* and not of the state or local authorities, the Supreme Court has no business telling state and local governments what to do with matters of religion. And, if one thought that, one would be correct," because the First Amendment

---

2. Quotes are from Stephen B. Presser, "The Ten Commandments Mish-Mosh," *American Spectator,* October 2005.

was adopted precisely to ensure that the federal government would not interfere with the established churches then in existence in several states.

So why did the Court enter this dangerous and apparently unconstitutional terrain? The simple answer is: because it wanted to. The justices who pioneered the role of the Supreme Court in adjudicating such cases found their opening in a controversial application of the Fourteenth Amendment. That amendment reads in part: "No State shall make or enforce any law which shall abridge the privileges or immunities of citizens of the United States; nor shall any State deprive any person of life, liberty, or property, without due process of law; nor deny to any person within its jurisdiction the equal protection of the laws." As Presser explains, the Court simply declared that the Fourteenth Amendment "somehow changed the meaning of the First Amendment so that *'Congress'* ought to be interpreted as meaning *'Any state or local governmental official.'*"

At this point we come face to face with the infamous "incorporation" doctrine that has become the avenue for a vast expansion of federal power and influence. Presser explains that this doctrine was an act of "judicial legerdemain" through which the Court simply dictated that limitations placed on the federal government by the Bill of Rights should also be understood as applying to state and local governments as well. This, he declares, "is one of the great constitutional usurpations of the modern era, but [it] now goes virtually unchallenged."

The Fourteenth Amendment was intended to provide no such opening for a vast expansion of federal power. Instead, it was, as Presser explains, originally designed as a safeguard for the contract and property rights of the newly freed slaves. So far, so good. Nevertheless, "the Supreme Court no longer feels itself bound by that history, and for many years the Fourteenth Amendment has been used by the Court as a tool to dictate what the states can and cannot do in matters of education, religion, abortion, gender, and a whole host of other areas completely unrelated to the original purposes of that provision."

This crucial chapter in American constitutional history is of tremendous importance. Most Americans remain blissfully unaware of the process whereby the federal government, through its judicial branch, now claims the right and power to determine issues that were never understood by the Founders to be within its purview.

The incorporation doctrine has not gone without criticism. As Presser indicates, Attorney General Edwin Meese publicly attacked the doctrine, only to experience a vitriolic assault. When it comes to the Court's decisions on matters of religion, this leaves the field wide open to those who would argue for the most thoroughly secular shape for America's public life.

In 2005 the Supreme Court "had an opportunity to resolve the status of the Decalogue in American public life," Presser explains, "but, alas, only sowed further confusion."

Presser provides a brilliant and concise summary of the two decisions:

 When the smoke cleared on the two Ten Commandments cases, the Court had held that the Commandments had to be removed from Kentucky courtrooms, but it was perfectly permissible for them to exist on a monolith outside the Texas legislature. There are nine members of the Supreme Court, and both of these cases were decided by 5–4 majorities. In each case, Justices Stevens, Souter, O'Connor, and Ginsburg wanted the Ten Commandments banned, and Justices Rehnquist, Scalia, Kennedy, and Thomas wanted them to stay. Justice Breyer believed the Texas display was fine, but the Kentucky ones were not, and, casting the deciding vote in both cases, his views prevailed. A review of the two cases illuminates the sad state of establishment clause jurisprudence in particular, and the general arbitrariness of a majority of the justices.

In his dissent to the Kentucky ruling, Justice Antonin Scalia cited an earlier decision and wrote, "We are a religious people whose institutions presuppose a Supreme Being." In his concurring opinion in the Texas case, Justice Clarence Thomas directly condemned the incorporation doctrine. Presser refers to Thomas's objection as "an acknowledgment as rare among justices as it is indisputable as a matter of history."

To his credit, Presser does not oversimplify the complexities of these cases. Instead, he simply asserts that the Court has unnecessarily compromised its own authority in delivering to the nation "this jurisprudential mish-mosh." Much of the confusion would be avoided if the justices interpreted the Constitution in terms of its original understanding. "Original understanding can't clear up everything in constitutional law," Presser admits, "but if the Court were more committed to interpreting the Constitution rather than social planning for the Republic, it might well diminish the number of 5–4 decisions rendered on important public issues." Presser's review of the Ten Commandments cases helps to clear the air, even as his historical analysis points to the intractable nature of the Court's misadventures.

Now when any case involving references to deity in the public square comes before the Court, the ground is clear for proponents of the most radical secularism to have their day. The only mitigating factor in these cases is the personal restraint exercised by at least some of the justices. Some argue that the only reason the Court has not adopted an even more pervasively secularist approach is fear of public outrage.

Intelligent Christians should look to these developments with concern and with determination to contend for
religious liberty. A fundamental and dangerous lie stands at
the very center of the secularist argument. If there is no
power higher than the state, then the state automatically
becomes the highest power on earth. This is a most dangerous assumption, and it opens the door to fascism and
unchecked assertions of state power.

From the very founding of this republic, presidents, justices, legislators, and citizens have insisted that the nation is
accountable to a higher power and a higher law. Of course,
many of the Founders were believing Christians. Those who
were not were generally deists of one variety or another,
united in their denial of raw state power and united in denying the ultimacy of the state. The secularist argument is
shipwrecked on the actual wording of the Constitution and
the unquestionable beliefs and practices of the Founders.

Yet there is a danger on the other side as well. Christians
must contend for religious liberty and for the right of citizens to express their deepest convictions and beliefs in the
public square. Furthermore, we should insist that the state
is not ultimate and that the state's actions and laws are
accountable to God. Nevertheless, we must be honest in
acknowledging that public and ceremonial references to
deity are not tantamount to statements of belief in the triune God—Father, Son, and Holy Spirit. The church bears
responsibility to preach and teach the gospel and to bear

witness, without compromise or governmental restraints, to the one true and living God. Likewise, the church should ask for no assistance from the state but should preach the gospel on the basis of its own identity, mission, and divine assignment. In other words, even as the U.S. Supreme Court produces a jurisprudence of confusion, the church is called to be a voice of clarity and truth.

7

ALL THAT TERROR TEACHES

Have We Learned Anything?

We are living in dangerous times, but far too many Americans seem to have forgotten this unforgiving fact. How can so many forget the unforgettable?

Terror is a tragic teacher, and the memories of September 11, 2001, haunt us even now. The images of planes crashing, towers collapsing, and bodies falling will be forever seared into our memories. Just to say "9/11" is to evoke a flood of remembrance and the bitter taste of tragedy.

A decade after the tragedy of 9/11, what have we learned? The immediate aftermath of the terror attacks in New York and Washington was widespread confusion. What had happened? Who was responsible? How awful is the damage? How many have died? Is more to come? The confusion gave way to even more terrifying clarity. The carnage was just too much to imagine—but too real to deny.

We know so much more now than we knew then. But have we really learned anything? We must hope so, but lessons learned in a moment of urgency have a way of fading into memory. What lessons must remain?

First, the terror has taught us to accept reality. This is a dangerous world. Towers we thought to be sound were attacked in a nation we thought to be safe, hit by airplanes we thought were no threat. Reality has a way of interrupting our dreams, and Americans have dreamed ourselves safe from the dangers that threaten the rest of the world. Those dreams came to an end on September 11. Americans now routinely accept levels of scrutiny and screening that would have baffled previous generations. We line up for airport security checks, taking off shoes and coats, while we send our earthly goods through x-ray machines and walk through metal detectors, all the while talking with friends and family as if this were normal—for now it is. How can people who board airplanes fail to remember that we live in a dangerous world?

Second, the terror has taught us to distinguish between good and evil. Our age has grown ever more reluctant to make moral judgments. Moral cowardice has denied the inherent evil of immoral acts. Moral relativism has denied any objective judgment of right and wrong. A naive nonjudgmentalism often masquerades as moral humility. But a refusal to make moral judgments is not humility. It is insanity.

The American university culture has embraced this false humility as a basic worldview. Speaking of morally disarmed college students, journalist David Brooks explained: "On campus they found themselves wrapped in a haze of relativism. There were words and jargon and ideas everywhere, but nothing solid that would allow a person to climb from one idea to the next. These students were trying to form judgments, yet were blocked by the accumulated habits of non-judgmentalism."[1]

These "accumulated habits of non-judgmentalism" are very much in evidence on America's campuses today and in the academic world of publishing and public lectures. Why would we expect moral sanity from a campus culture that celebrates Michael Moore, Alec Baldwin, and Noam Chomsky as wise men?

Yet these habits of non-judgmentalism were of no use on September 11. The attacks on New York and Washington, carefully planned to maximize civilian casualties and terror, were unadulterated evil. These were not acts of cultural rebellion or national liberation. They were acts of murderous terror at the hands of men rightly named as murderous terrorists. We came face to face with the undeniable reality of

---

1. David Brooks, "War and Man at Yale," *Daily Standard* online, October 29, 2001.

evil. Moral relativism was stripped of its disguise on September 11. It is evil to speak of those attacks as anything less than evil.

Third, we learned once again that God is ultimately in control, or else we are lost in a cosmos of chaos. Tragedy breeds theological tremors. Is God really in control? Could a good God allow such pain and loss? Can we really know anything about God at all? Christians were called upon to answer these questions with the calm confidence of biblical truth and genuine faith. God has revealed Himself in the Bible, and He has shown Himself to be both omnipotent and loving. Both truths are nonnegotiable, and each complements the other. We have no choice but to affirm both of them as two sides of one great truth and to affirm that God's sovereignty and His moral perfection are established in His own revelation and in His own terms.

Fourth, we were reminded that the gospel itself has enemies. We should have known this all along, for the apostle Paul described the gospel of Christ's Cross as a stumbling block and scandal. The Cross has its enemies. The attacks of 9/11 were made in the name of Islam—not in the name of secularism. Muslim and non-Muslim alike argued whether Islam is at war with America or if the terrorists were acting in violation of the Koran. Whatever the merits of those arguments, the more important truth is that, at a level far beyond any recent geopolitical developments, the religion of Islam is at war with the Cross of Christ. Those who love the gospel must be reminded that Islam rejects Christ as the incarnate Son of God and the Cross as the atonement for our salvation. There ultimately can be no reconciliation between the claims of Christianity and the claims of Islam. The enemies of the Cross know this full well.

Secularism raised its head in the aftermath of 9/11 to warn that anyone who takes truth claims seriously is a potential terrorist—the Christian as well as the Muslim. Claims that Jesus is the only Savior and that salvation is found in His name alone were dismissed as "theological terrorism" and religious extremism. But it was for this very claim that the early Christian martyrs gave their lives.

Fifth, we learned that spirituality is no substitute for Christian faith. Churches were filled to capacity in the weeks following September 11. Some observers predicted a period of national revival and openness to the gospel. That did not happen. Within just a few months, church attendance had fallen to pre-9/11 levels. The national trauma produced flutterings of spirituality but little evidence of renewed Christian conviction.

Spirituality is what is left when authentic Christianity is evacuated from the public square. It is the refuge of the faithless seeking the trappings of faith without the demands of revealed truth. Spirituality affirms us in our self-centeredness and soothingly tells us that all is well. Authentic faith in Christ calls us out of ourselves, points us to the Cross, and summons us to follow Christ.

The lessons terror taught us are still fresh for those with the will to remember. The gaping hole in Manhattan's skyline and the memories of Washington's scarred landscape point to the unspeakably greater loss measured in human life and human misery. The distance of years has not healed the wounds, but it has sharpened the memory. There are lessons we have learned. In the midst of a very different war, the indomitable G. K. Chesterton understood the same lessons.

From all that terror teaches,
From lies of tongue and pen,
From all the easy speeches
That comfort cruel men,
From sale and profanation
Of honour and the sword,
From sleep and from damnation,
Deliver us, good Lord!

G. K. Chesterton
"A Hymn"

8

NEEDED: AN EXIT STRATEGY FROM PUBLIC SCHOOLS

The Crisis Christian Parents Face

Christian parents are increasingly aware that the public schools are prime battlegrounds for cultural conflict. Given the deep ideological chasm that separates the worldviews and expectations of many educators from those held by many parents, we should not be surprised by the vitriolic nature of this conflict.

That said, recent developments indicate that the public schools will soon be even more hostile to the convictions of many Christian families. Just ask Rob and Robin Wirthlin, parents of a seven-year-old student at Joseph Estabrook Elementary School in Lexington, Massachusetts. The Wirthlins' son came home talking about a school lesson based on the book *King & King*—a parable about homosexual marriage. In the story, the young prince decides that he wants to marry the one he loves, who happens to be another prince.

"My son is only 7 years old," this concerned mother remarked. "By presenting this kind of issue at such a young age, they're trying to indoctrinate our children. They're intentionally presenting this as a norm, and it's not a value that our family supports."

That same school district was roiled by controversy just months before when another parent, David Parker, complained that his son, a first-grader, had been taught about families with same-sex parents and sent home with a "diversity book bag." The lesson? The children were taught that there are no normal families, and that all family structures are equally valid. Those who think otherwise are lacking in appreciation for—you guessed it—family diversity.

Look closely at the response of Paul Ash, the Lexington school superintendent, to the concerns of these parents: "We couldn't run a public school system if every parent who feels some topic is objectionable to them for moral or religious reasons decides their child should be removed.... Lexington is committed to teaching children about the world they live in, and in Massachusetts same-sex marriage is legal."[1]

Massachusetts law requires that parents be advised in advance when issues of sexuality are to be discussed. They can then "opt-out" their children from these lessons. But school administrators insist that lessons about family structure—even those dealing with same-sex marriage—are exempt from this requirement. Thus far, they are standing on their policy. Parents who have children in this school district will just have to accept the lessons or remove their children from the public schools altogether.

These examples are not isolated exceptions to the rule. More and more, they reflect what is happening in America's public schools. Some parents find this out when their children come home reporting that a teacher who was one sex when they started the school year is now the opposite sex. Concerned parents are told to just deal with it. Older students are exposed to the national "Day of Silence," an observance that is organized by homosexual activists and has spread to thousands of American public high schools.

On top of all this, recent court decisions have added momentum to the trend and seriously undermined parental

---

1. Tracy Jan, "Parents Rip School over Gay Storybook," *Boston Globe,* April 20, 2006. www.boston.com/news/local/articles/2006/04/20/parents_rip_school_over_gay_storybook.

rights. In 2005 a three-judge panel on the U.S. Court of Appeals for the Ninth Circuit handed down a decision that denied California parents the right to block their children from being asked sexually explicit questions on questionnaires. The case in question, *Fields v. Palmdale School District,* dealt with the fact that children in grades one through three were asked questions about such things as "getting scared or upset when I think about sex," "having sex feelings in my body," and "touching my private parts too much."

In the panel's unanimous decision, written by Judge Stephen Reinhardt, the court held "that there is no fundamental right of parents to be the exclusive provider of information regarding sexual matters to their children, either independent of their right to direct the upbringing and education of their children or encompassed by it."[2]

Remember that the children in question were as young as five years old. California's parents were bluntly told that they have "no fundamental right" to be the exclusive sex educators of their own young children. In the eyes of many parents, asking those invasive questions of children that young is tantamount to child abuse.

Make no mistake—there is a clear agenda here. Issues of sexuality and diversity may take the headlines, but a host of other issues is also at stake. Generations of progressivist

---

2. *Fields v. Palmdale School District,* 427 F.3rd 1197; 2005 V.S. App. Lexis 23643 (November 2, 2005).

educators, driven by the assumption that they—not parents—know what is best for America's children, have been busy shaping textbooks, curricula, and school policies.

Beyond this, groups such as the National Education Association, the leading union for public-school teachers, have a virtual stranglehold on many school districts. Decisions about school curricula and policies are increasingly set by bureaucracies far removed from local control.

The crisis in public-school education has prompted some to reconsider the very idea of public education. Some now argue that Christian parents cannot send their children to public schools without committing the sin of handing their children over to a pagan and ungodly system. Fueled by a secularist agenda and influenced by an elite of radical educational bureaucrats and theorists, government schools now serve as engines for secularizing and radicalizing children.

A look at the historical background is instructive. The public-school system in America has been controversial at various turns in our national history—but never as now. The government's early involvement in education was part of the young nation's effort to create an educated citizenry that would be truly democratic. Education was not to be limited to an elitist group of wealthy Americans, but was to be made available to all.

In the early twentieth century, another purpose entered the picture. Vast waves of immigration, primarily from Europe, brought millions of Irish, Italian, German, and other

European families to America. Educational leaders like John Dewey saw the public schools, often called the "common" schools, as the mechanism for indoctrinating children into a new democratic faith. The worldviews and eccentricities of the various ethnic and national backgrounds would be erased and a new melting pot of Americans would emerge. Dewey, the most influential shaper of the public schools in America, understood that the success of his effort would require children to be liberated from the prejudices and values of their parents.

In his book *A Common Faith,* Dewey advocated a radically secular vision for the public schools and the larger public culture. His concept of a humanistic faith, stripped of all supernatural claims, doctrines, and theological authorities, would replace Christianity as the dominant, culture-shaping worldview. "Here are all the elements for a religious faith that shall not be confined to sect, class, or race," he claimed. "Such a faith has always been the common faith of mankind. It remains for us to make it explicit and militant."[3]

It has taken longer than Dewey expected, but this secularist faith is certainly explicit and militant now. Of course, this is not equally true in all places and in all public schools. As a rule, the effects of this educational revolution are less evident in schools in more rural areas, with local political

---

3. John Dewey, *A Common Faith* (New Haven: Yale University Press, 1962), 87.

control more concentrated in the hands of parents. In some school systems, the majority of teachers, administrators, and students share an outlook that is at least friendly and respectful toward Christianity and conservative moral values.

In other places, the situation is markedly different. In many metropolitan school districts, the schools have truly become engines for the indoctrination of the young. This process of indoctrination pervades, not only the more recognizable aspects of radical sex education programs and so-called health education, but other aspects of the curriculum as well. Unless something revolutionary reverses these trends, this is the shape of the future.

With control over the public-school system increasingly in the hands of the courts, educational bureaucrats, the university-based education schools, and the powerful teachers' unions, little hope for correction appears. Federal mandates, accreditation requirements, union demands, and the influence of the educational elite represent a combined force that is far greater than the localized influence of many school boards, not to mention parents. Those who doubt the radical commitments of groups such as the National Education Association should simply look at the organization's public statements, policy positions, and initiatives.

The breakdown of the public-school system is a national tragedy. An honest assessment of the history of public education in America must acknowledge the success of the common school vision in breaking down ethnic, economic, and racial barriers. The schools have brought hundreds of millions of American children into a democracy of common citizenship. Tragically, that vision was displaced by an ideologically driven attempt to force a radically secular worldview.

So, what should Christian parents and churches do? I am convinced that the time has come for Christians to develop an exit strategy from the public schools. Some parents made this decision long ago. The Christian school and home school movements are among the most significant cultural developments of the last thirty years. Other parents are not there yet. In any event, an exit strategy should be in place.

This strategy would affirm the basic and ultimate responsibility of Christian parents to take charge of the education of their own children. The strategy would also affirm the responsibility of churches to equip parents, support families, and offer alternatives. At the same time, this strategy must acknowledge that Christian churches, families, and parents do not yet see the same realities, the same threats, and the same challenges in every context. Sadly, this is almost certainly just a matter of time.

Meanwhile, the parade of shocking headlines continues, and millions of American children—including many from Christian homes—are being taught at school what would never be taught at home. Some major point of crisis is likely to bring all this to an end. The only question is when.

9

THE GOD GENE

Bad Science Meets
Bad Theology

S ociobiologist Edward O. Wilson once declared religious belief to be "the greatest challenge to human sociobiology and its most exciting opportunity to progress as a truly original theoretical discipline."[1] In other words, Wilson admitted that belief in God is a fundamental challenge to the theory of evolution, since evolution cannot explain why this belief could be so widespread, so powerful, and so closely tied to human existence. Now, Dean Hamer, a geneticist at the National Cancer Institute at the National Institutes of Health, claims to have found the genetic

---

1. Edward O. Wilson, *On Human Nature* (Cambridge, MA: Harvard University Press, 2004), 175. First published in 1978.

explanation for belief in God—a "God gene" that provides an evolutionary explanation for faith.

Dean Hamer's work, published as *The God Gene: How Faith Is Hardwired into Our Genes,* has attracted considerable attention. His argument that belief in God is tied to a mix of factors, but localized in a specific gene, fits the reductionistic mind of the age. Furthermore, Hamer's hypothesis is the natural complement to a purely materialistic worldview.

The evolutionary worldview leads to a specific understanding of the human being, and that understanding is derived directly from pure materialism. The human being is understood to be the product of an evolutionary process that at every point is explained purely in terms of natural factors. Humans are collections of atoms and molecules, and all consciousness, belief, emotion, and moral judgment must be explained by nothing more than biochemical processes within the brain. In other words, the evolutionary mind-set must reject the notion of a soul and must insist that all dimensions of consciousness are definable in purely physical terms.

In the physicalist worldview, the entire human experience is explained by genes, chemicals, natural selection, and the environment. In *The God Gene,* Hamer attempts to explain religion and spirituality in purely physical terms. Yet before he ever discusses the so-called God gene, he redefines faith itself. Hamer begins his book with an illustration drawn from Buddhist spirituality, and within the first ten pages he redefines faith as "self-transcendence." As he explains, "Self-transcendence provides a numerical measure of people's capacity to reach out beyond themselves—to see everything in the world as part of one great totality. If I were to describe it in a single word, it might be 'at-one-ness.'"[2]

Hamer admits that self-transcendence will sound a bit "flaky" to many readers. Nevertheless, "it successfully passes the test for a solid psychological trait." Well, at least it passes the test of serving as a useful tool that will enable Hamer to continue his argument.

Continuing in a New Age direction, Hamer distinguishes "spirituality" from "religion." Spirituality is tied to his notion of self-transcendence, while religion is far more concrete, rational, and particular. As Hamer explains, "The self-transcendence scale tries to separate one's spirituality from one's particular religious beliefs by eschewing questions about belief in a particular God, frequency of prayer, or orthodox religious doctrines or practices." Just in case we missed the point, Hamer adds: "Even individuals who dislike all forms of organized religion may have a strong spiritual capacity and score high on the self-transcendent scale." So…the God gene doesn't actually have anything directly to do with believing in God, Hamer argues, but only with the capacity to achieve self-transcendence.[3]

Once Hamer makes this argument, he surrenders any

2. Dean Hamer, *The God Gene: How Faith Is Hardwired into Our Genes* (New York: Anchor, 2004), 10.
3. Hamer, *The God Gene*, 10.

sense of integrity in talking about a God gene. Having redefined his terms, limiting the specific scope of his explanatory
thesis to concern for self-transcendence that can be understood in purely secular terms, Hamer undermines his own
argument and marketing strategy.

Since Hamer is a research scientist who hopes to maintain some credibility in the scientific community, he must
offer several qualifications to his work. First, Hamer acknowledges that a genetic explanation can go only so far in explaining the totality of religious experience, or even self-
transcendence. "The specific gene I have identified is by no
means the entire story behind spirituality," Hamer admits.
"It plays only a small, if key, role; many other genes and
environmental factors also are involved. Nevertheless, the
gene is important because it points out the mechanism by
which spirituality is manifested in the brain."[4]

Before considering Hamer's genetic argument, what are
we to make of his category of self-transcendence? Hamer
uses the term to mean "spiritual feelings that are independent of traditional religiousness." These feelings are not tied
to belief in any specific god, nor are they tied to traditional
practices of devotion or to any doctrinal structure. Instead,
self-transcendence "gets to the heart of spiritual belief: the
nature of the universe and our place in it." Individuals who
experience self-transcendence "tend to see everything,

---

4. Hamer, *The God Gene*, 11.

including themselves, as part of one great totality."[5] In other words, they sound like individuals who have graduated from the latest New Age self-help course in spirituality.

A central mechanism of Hamer's argument is a self-transcendence scale devised by psychiatrist Robert Cloninger of the School of Medicine at Washington University in St. Louis. Cloninger's instrument for measuring self-transcendence, known as a "temperament and character inventory (TCI)," provides Hamer with a way of establishing a research base in which he could study twins in order to determine whether belief in God is a heritable characteristic.

Fast-forwarding Hamer's argument, he claims to have discovered a gene known as VMAT2, which controls the flow of monoamines within the brain. Monoamines are chemicals in the brain that can make us feel pleasurable, ecstatic, or depressed. Monoamines include dopamine and serotonin and are customarily released by psychotropic drugs and hallucinogenics. Thus, Hamer argues that evolution explains why many individuals possess the VMAT2 gene and are thus more likely to have their monoamines regulated in a way that leads to self-transcendence. Following so far?

Once self-transcendence is defined as the goal of this evolutionary process, and once VMAT2 is identified as the gene responsible for creating the feelings associated with self-transcendence, Hamer is well on his way to arguing that

---

5. Hamer, *The God Gene*, 18.

self-transcendence plays a role in evolution by fostering optimism in individuals possessing the trait. Such optimism leads to better health, to a more positive outlook toward the future, and increased likelihood that these individuals will have children and hand down their genes through the biological process.

This physicalist explanation, limiting something like faith in God to purely chemical factors, is necessary because Hamer and his colleagues are committed materialists. He explicitly admits this fact in *The God Gene*. Insisting that a scientific explanation for belief in God must be expressed in terms of chemistry and physics, Hamer explains: "Proponents of this view often are called 'materialists' because they believe that all mental processes can ultimately be accounted for by a few basic physical laws. Most scientists, including myself, are materialists."[6]

In other words, as a committed materialist, Dean Hamer is looking for an explanation of belief in God that will fit his evolutionary worldview. In order to do this, he has to jettison all that is customarily associated with theism, avoid everything that has to do with the content of belief, and redefine his entire concern in terms of self-transcendence—an experience he admits can be purely secular. In other words, Dean Hamer tells us absolutely nothing about belief in God and very little about modern genetics.

---

6. Hamer, *The God Gene*, 94.

This point was made devastatingly clear in a review of *The God Gene* published in the October 2004 issue of *Scientific American*. Carl Zimmer, another major evolutionary theorist, blasts *The God Gene* as bad science and reckless argument. As Zimmer notes, this is not the first time a scientist has tried to prove a genetic basis for some human behavior. "In 1993, for example, a scientist reported a genetic link to male homosexuality in a region of the X chromosome. The report brought a huge media fanfare, but other scientists who tried to replicate the study failed. The scientist's name was Dean Hamer."

That's right. Dean Hamer is most famously (or infamously) known for his claim to have found a genetic explanation for male homosexuality. That study created a firestorm in the press, and though it was never replicated in order to establish scientific credibility, it quickly became standard fare for arguments claiming homosexuality to be absolutely natural, and therefore normal.

As Zimmer laments, "Given the fate of Hamer's so-called gay gene, it is strange to see him so impatient to trumpet the discovery of his God gene." Zimmer then turns the table on Hamer, arguing that *The God Gene* should have been titled "*A Gene That Accounts for Less Than One Percent of the Variance Found in Scores on Psychological Questionnaires Designed to Measure a Factor Called Self-Transcendence, Which Can Signify Everything from Belonging to the Green Party to Believing in ESP, According to One Unpublished,*

Unreplicated Study."[7] In the scientific community, that's undiluted condemnation.

It is laughable to suggest that belief in God is tied to any genetic structure that can be accounted for in this way. The Bible provides an authoritative explanation for our capacity to know God. As the book of Genesis makes clear, human beings are made in the image of God. It is the *imago dei* that explains the fact that we are the only creatures consciously able to know God, and to know Him intimately.

Any effort to create a genetic explanation for a generic experience of self-transcendence will fall far short of scientific credibility. More important, it will fall tragically short of providing an adequate theological explanation for how human creatures can know our Creator. That explanation is found only within the Bible, and it is itself a knowledge revealed to us by our Creator.

The God Gene is a parable for our postmodern times, further evidence of the lengths to which clever humans will go in trying to deny that we were made by a Creator who designed us with the capacity to know Him. Hamer's book is bad science and bad theology combined, but it does succeed in making one point clear: materialism just can't answer the big questions.

---

7. Carl Zimmer, "Faith-Boosting Genes," *Scientific American,* October 2004, www.sciam.com/article.cfm?articleID=000AD4E7-6290-1150-902F83414B7F4945&pageNumber=1&catID=2.

10

ARE WE RAISING A NATION OF WIMPS?

A Coddled Generation Cannot Cope

To be honest, I look at the magazine *Psychology Today* as something of a trade journal for the therapeutic culture. The magazine spins out seemingly endless cover stories on how to be happy, self-actualized, and successful, but its worldview is light-years from classical Bible-based Christianity. Nevertheless, *Psychology Today* is really onto something with its article "A Nation of Wimps," written by Hara Estroff Marano.[1] This article is must reading for every parent.

Marano begins her article with a portrait of cushioned

---

1. All quotes in this chapter are from Hara Estroff Marano, "A Nation of Wimps," *Psychology Today*, November–December 2004, 58–70, 103. Accessed at http://psychologytoday.com/articles/pto-3584.html.

childhood. "Maybe it's the cyclist in the park, trim under his sleek metallic blue helmet, cruising along the dirt path…at three miles an hour. On his tricycle." From there, Marano moves to cite the "all-rubber-cushioned surface where kids used to skin their knees" and the fact that the kids aren't even allowed to play alone. Their mommies and daddies are playing with them, making sure that the little darlings don't experience even the slightest scrape, scratch, or scare. "Few take it half-easy on the perimeter benches, as parents used to do," Marano explains, "letting the kids figure things out for themselves."

To the contrary, today's parents are now spending a great deal of their time doing little more than protecting their children from life. Marano describes this as "the wholly sanitized childhood, without skinned knees or the occasional C in history." The result of all this? Our kids are growing up to be pampered wimps who are incapable of assuming adult responsibility and have no idea how to handle the routine challenges of life.

David Elkind, a prominent child psychologist, counters, "Kids need to feel badly sometimes.… We learn through experience and we learn through bad experiences. Through failure we learn how to cope."

That seems to be a foreign concept to many of today's parents. Coddled by a generation of baby boomers, today's parents have turned into hyperprotectors. Kids are not allowed to play, because they might get hurt. In today's highly competitive environment, kids have to excel at everything, even if parents have to actually do the work or negotiate an assisted success. The routine play of childhood—even the pointless chatter, nonsense, and aimless play of children—is now considered wasted time or worse. "Messing up" is simply out of style, Marano explains. "Although error and experimentation are the true mothers of success, parents are taking pains to remove failure from the equation."

"Whether we want to or not, we're on our way to creating a nation of wimps," Marano warns. She fast-forwards to college and university campuses, where the "fragility factor" is now most clearly evident. As she explains, "It's where intellectual and developmental tracks converge as the emotional training wheels come off. By all accounts, psychological distress is rampant on college campuses."

This statement is easily verified by observing the reports issued by academic institutions. Psychological distress—sometimes evident in the mild form of anxiety and, in other cases, in binge drinking, self-mutilation, and even suicide—are now major concerns of college administrators.

As Steven Hyman, Harvard University's provost and former director of the National Institute of Mental Health lamented, the problem "is interfering with the core mission of the university." What is the source of this problem? Observers are zeroing in on parental pampering as the most critical factor behind this pattern of student "disconnect." Smothered by parental attention and decision making during childhood and adolescence, these young people arrive on college campuses without the ability to make their own decisions, live with their choices, learn from their experiences, and grapple with the issues of adult life.

But the academic issues do not show up only on college campuses. Today's kids must be successful, at least in the view of their insistent parents. Even in prekindergarten programs, parents now show up with a list of special demands, insisting that their child must be treated with special care. Inevitably, this is often transformed into diagnoses of learning disabilities that will require special instructional accommodations. If this trend is not reversed, virtually all students will be diagnosed with some form of learning disability, and the entire classroom experience will break down. Marano blames this on parental "hyperconcern."

John Portmann, professor of religious studies at the University of Virginia, suggests that American parents "expect their children to be perfect—the smartest, fastest, most charming people in the universe. And if they can't get their children to prove it on their own, they'll turn to doctors to make their kids into the people that parents want to believe their kids are." Inevitably, what the parents are actually doing, Portmann stresses, is "showing kids how to work the system for their own benefit."

By the time these kids get to college, some parents are just getting warmed up. "Talk to a college president or administrator," Marano advises, "and you're almost certainly bound to hear tales of the parents who call at 2 a.m. to protest Brandon's C in economics because it's going to damage his shot at grad school."

The article goes on to cite the experience of psychologist Robert Epstein of the University of California, San Diego. When Epstein announced to his class that he "expected them to work hard and would hold them to high standards," he received an outraged response from a parent—using his official judicial stationery—accusing the professor of mistreating the young. Epstein, himself a former editor in chief of *Psychology Today*, later filed a complaint with the California Commission on Judicial Performance, and the judge was censured by that body for abusing his office. Nevertheless, this is just one more incident in what is becoming a normal experience on too many campuses.

How special are today's students? Well, according to their report cards and diplomas, they are very special. The problem of grade inflation now means that, in terms of an actual measure of academic excellence, grades are now virtually useless. On some campuses, the average grade is approaching an A. Lawrence Summers, former president of Harvard University, discovered when he assumed the university's presidency in 2001 that 94 percent of the college's graduates were graduating with honors. Peter Stearns of George Mason University argues that grade inflation "is the institutional response to parental anxiety about school demands on children." As Marano expands, "It is a pure index of emotional over-investment in a child's success."

In an interesting twist, Marano focuses on one particular technology that hampers the ability of today's children to establish their own identity and responsible decision making—the cell phone. "Even in college—or perhaps especially at college—students are typically in contact with their parents several times a day, reporting every flicker of experience," Marano observes. When parents play along with this dependency, they "infantalize" their children, "keeping them in a permanent state of dependency." Life is lived in an endless present tense, with no need to frame long-term decisions, make plans, or engage in sustained interpersonal conversations.

Who is at fault here? Marano presents this situation as rooted in bad parenting and the unwillingness of parents to allow their children to fail. Undoubtedly, this is part of the problem. Today's parents often see their children as little trophies to be polished. Many see life as a competitive game, and they are determined to do whatever it takes to get their children on top—even if it means cutting corners, changing the rules, and even writing little Johnny's term papers. No doubt, Marano is onto something here. As one college student lamented to his counselor, "I wish my parents had some hobby other than me."

David Anderegg, a professor at Bennington College,

warns that parents must not try to protect their children from life. "If you have an infant and the baby has gas, burping the baby is being a good parent," he explains. "But when you have a 10-year-old who has metaphoric gas, you don't have to burp him. You have to let him sit with it, try to figure out what to do about it. He then learns to tolerate moderate amounts of difficulty, and it's not the end of the world."

Christian parents can fall into this same game, pushing our children as if worldly markers of success are to be our greatest goals and hallmarks of achievement. We must push our children toward excellence, but we must define excellence in biblical terms consistent with the Christian gospel. Our concern should be that our children are raised in the nurture and admonition of the Lord and are pointed to God's purpose for their life. A life spent in self-sacrificial service, on the mission field, or devoted to the cause of the gospel will not win the plaudits of the world.

Marano's article should serve to warn us all that we must not protect our children from the process of growing into adulthood. While we are charged to protect our children from evil and to guard them from harm, we are not to shield them from reality. As our children grow older, they should demonstrate an increasing maturity that allows them to deal with the problems of life—not to run from them.

Beyond this, we must expand our concern to the young people as well as their parents. Without doubt, hyper-attentive parents who coddle their children are part of the

problem. Nevertheless, we also face the reality of a generation that seems, in all too many cases, unwilling to grow up,
assume responsibility, and become genuine adults.

Hara Estroff Marano's article is a bracing alert addressed
to today's generation of parents. This article demands our
attention, even as Christians will want to press its arguments
further. Let's be thankful for the lessons learned from
skinned knees, routine disappointments, and hard work.
Otherwise, we too will be raising a generation of wimps.

11

HARD AMERICA, SOFT AMERICA

The Battle for America's Future

Anyone who cares about politics in America knows who Michael Barone is and recognizes him as the ultimate political junkie's junkie. In addition to his other responsibilities, Barone serves as "principal coauthor" of *The Almanac of American Politics,* the indispensable reference guide to the nation's political order, which is published every two years. Barone is nothing less than a Fort Knox of political information. Like a baseball fanatic who can roll off batting averages from eighty years ago, Barone knows American politics in such detail that he can usually talk about individual congressional districts with great insight and accuracy. When it comes to the data of American politics, if Michael Barone does not know it, it probably cannot be known.

Yet Barone's book *Hard America, Soft America* really isn't about American politics—at least not directly. In this book, Barone offers an illuminating analysis into the real division that marks the American cultural landscape. As he sees it, Americans are torn between two poles of cultural energy— between *hardness* and *softness* as the texture of the society.

Barone begins by looking with admiration at the young men and women of the American armed services who fought with such spectacular success in Afghanistan and Iraq. These young soldiers were incredibly competent, marked by fierce resolve, and characterized by great personal discipline. But as Barone reflected, "I could not help thinking also that only a few years earlier these enlisted men and women, and not so many years earlier these officers and noncommissioned officers, were more or less typical American adolescents." As he continued, "For many years I have thought it one of the peculiar features of our country that we seem to produce incompetent eighteen-year-olds but remarkably competent thirty-year-olds."[1]

How does this happen? Barone explains that American youngsters "live mostly in what I call Soft America—the parts of our country where there is little competition and

---

1. Michael Barone, *Hard America, Soft America* (New York: Three Rivers, 2005), 12.

accountability."[2] But once these adolescents emerge into adulthood and have to work for a living in a competitive economy, they find themselves in "Hard America," where competition and accountability are the rules of the day.

Barone sets out his distinction between Hard America and Soft America with clarity. "Soft America coddles: our schools, seeking to instill self-esteem, ban tag and dodgeball, and promote just about anyone who shows up. Hard America plays for keeps: the private sector fires people when profits fall, and the military trains under live fire." Clearly, Barone believes that hardness is necessary for the preservation and protection of society and the training of young people into the responsibilities of adulthood. He does not argue that all softness is bad, noting that we shouldn't "want to subject kindergartners to the rigors of the Marine Corps or leave old people helpless and uncared for."[3]

Barone believes that Soft America offers inadequate preparation for life, adulthood, and national destiny. He places the blame for this at the feet of intellectual elites pushing what historian Robert Wiebe called "bureaucratic" ideas.[4] Pragmatist philosopher John Dewey, whose ideas of "progressivist" education have warped the American educational establishment for almost a century, comes under

---

2. Barone, *Hard America, Soft America,* 13.
3. Barone, *Hard America, Soft America,* 13–15.
4. See, for example, Robert H. Wiebe, *The Search for Order, 1877–1920* (New York: Hill and Wang, 1967).

particular critique. As Dewey looked to the public schools, he saw an opportunity for the transformation of society. Rather than focusing on "book learning," testing, and personal competition, Dewey wanted to transform the schools into laboratories for social experimentation, nurturing children into life responsibilities and intellectual play. Instead of being guided by an authoritarian teacher, Dewey argued, children should be allowed to direct their own learning.

Much of the impetus toward a softening of American culture came in response to the robber barons and the fierce capitalism of the early twentieth century. Franklin D. Roosevelt's New Deal programs represented a softening of life for many Americans, shifting much of the economic responsibility of the nation from individuals to the state.

As Barone demonstrates, the nation has moved back and forth between periods of intense hardness and softness. The successful Soviet launch of the *Sputnik* satellite led Americans to demand an immediate hardening of public education. As Barone indicates, the impact of the National Defense Education Act, passed in 1958, was evident in significantly increased Scholastic Aptitude Test (SAT) scores in the early and mid-1960s.

Nevertheless, this hardening of the educational curriculum did not last long, for the academic elites demanded increased softening and pushed a liberal agenda that once again looked to the schools as laboratories for social experimentation and the coddling of young people. As educational historian Diane Ravitch explains, the school curricula of the late 1960s and early 1970s reflected a loosening of standards, the marginalization of classical disciplines, and the substitution of grade inflation and social promotion for achievement.[5] Leading educational theorists substituted a concern for self-esteem for learning, testing, and academic achievement. All this leaves most young Americans unprepared for the real demands of adulthood. "The stubborn resistance to hardening America's schools helps account for the fact that Americans up to age eighteen live mostly in Soft America," Barone argues, "just as most Americans after the age of eighteen live in Hard America."

Like the schools, the criminal justice system also became representative of Soft America. Criminals were increasingly not held accountable for their crimes, and "a broad swath of Americans who no longer felt morally justified in imposing hard penalties on crime deliberately and substantially softened the criminal justice system." Barone even argues that the war in Vietnam was a "soft war" because America's fighting forces were prevented from applying winning strategies and battle-hardened experience to the conflict, while politicians forced them to fight a mostly "defensive" war. By the 1980s and 1990s, Americans were increasingly frustrated with the failures of Soft America. Fed up with rising crime

5. Diane Ravitch, *Left Back: A Century of Failed School Reforms* (New York: Simon and Schuster, 2000).

rates, Americans elected political leaders such as Ronald Reagan and Rudy Giuliani, who called for tougher penalties, more police, and a more confrontational fight against crime.

As Barone sees it, the big question for America's future is whether the nation will move in a harder or a softer direction. This means a choice between competition and coddling, between therapy and truth, between concern for self-esteem and pride in genuine achievement. Applying his skills of political and cultural analysis, Barone sees a hardening in America's future.

Chastened by the terrorist attacks of September 11, 2001, has America been awakened out of its softness? Do Americans still have sufficient moral resolve to face the threat of world terrorism and the hard political, economic, and moral decisions of the present age? How we answer these questions in the coming years will tell us much about who we really are and what we really believe. One way or another, we will see a clearer vision of our future.

12

THE POST-TRUTH ERA

Welcome to the Age
of Dishonesty

Have we now reached a stage of social evolution that is
"beyond honesty"? That fascinating question is raised
by author Ralph Keyes in his book *The Post-Truth Era: Dishonesty and Deception in Contemporary Life.* "I think it's fair
to say that honesty is on the ropes," Keyes observes. "Deception has become commonplace at all levels of contemporary
life."[1] By the time you finish reading *The Post-Truth Era,*
Keyes is likely to have convinced you that dishonesty is now
the order of the day and that deception has now been insti-
tutionalized at virtually every level of American culture.

Keyes is an author of keen perception and wide-ranging

---

1. Ralph Keyes, *The Post-Truth Era: Dishonest and Deception in Contemporary Life* (New York: St. Martin's, 2004), 5.

observation. He has pulled together an enormous body of evidence, all pointing to the pervasive rise of dishonesty in American life. As Jeremy Campbell remarked in *The Liar's Tale*, "It is a creeping assumption at the start of a new millennium that there are things more important than truth."[2]

Keyes acknowledges that human beings have lied in the past, but he suggests that the current generation of liars has developed a skillfulness and nuance in lying that is virtually unprecedented in the human experience. "Even though there have always been liars, lies have usually been told with hesitation, a dash of anxiety, a bit of guilt, a little shame, at least some sheepishness," Keyes notes. "Now, clever people that we are, we have come up with rationales for tampering with truth so we can dissemble guilt-free."[3]

Keyes has a label for this new age of dishonesty. "I call it post-truth. We live in a post-truth era." Keyes credits the late Steve Tesich with coining this phrase, but Keyes now applies it with vigor to our contemporary culture. "Post-truthfulness exists in an ethical twilight zone," he explains. "It allows us to dissemble without considering ourselves dishonest." Since we do not want to think of ourselves as unethical, we simply "devise alternative approaches to morality."

As evidence of this cultural acceptance of lying, Keyes

---

2. Jeremy Campbell, *The Liar's Tale: A History of Falsehood* (New York: Norton, 2001).

3. Keyes, *The Post-Truth Era*, 12–13.

notes the rise of euphemisms for deception. "We no longer tell lies. Instead we 'misspeak.' We 'exaggerate.' We 'exercise poor judgment.' 'Mistakes were made,' we say. The term 'deceive' gives way to the more playful 'spin.' At worst, saying 'I wasn't truthful' sounds better than 'I lied.'" What are we to do with terms such as "poetic truth," "nuanced truth," "alternative reality," or "strategic misrepresentations"? In our technological age, driven by a digitalized dimension of lying, we are now accustomed to talking about "virtual truth." Keyes suggests that the use of such euphemisms is a new cultural syndrome he identifies as "euphemasia." This would include everything from terms such as "credibility gap" to Winston Churchill's "terminological inexactitudes."[4]

In a fascinating section, Keyes traces the history of lying. He suggests that early civilizations depended on honesty, at least within the kinship group, for the establishment of stable order and trust. Once society becomes more complicated and diverse, however, lying becomes more routine. In some cultures, lying to an enemy or a stranger is not considered immoral at all.

In more modern eras, lying was raised to a higher art form. In the history of Protestant confessionalism, creeds were to be accepted "without hesitation or mental reservation." This language continues among confessional Christians, who may wonder how the term *mental reservation*

---

4. Keyes, *The Post-Truth Era,* 13.

emerged in the first place. Keyes traces the use of mental reservation back to the Reformation era, when Catholics developed mental reservation as a defense for telling an untruth under threat of persecution. In time, however, the device of mental reservation allowed an individual to rationalize dishonesty, to hold or "reserve" the truth to himself even as he misled an interrogator. Before long, others used this excuse in order to give apparent assent to creedal statements while privately rejecting the very truths articulated in the statement of faith.

Just how important is honesty, after all? "Honesty's market value is too little appreciated in the history of ethics," Keyes argues.[5] Without honesty, there can be no confidence in legal contracts, no shared confidence in social arrangements, and no authority for the rule of law. As argued by Enlightenment philosopher Immanuel Kant, a healthy society can't remain healthy so long as it accepts lies. "For a lie always harms another," Kant asserted, "if not some other particular man, still it harms mankind generally, for it vitiates the source of law itself."[6]

Is lying a symptom of social pathology? Keyes considers the argument that social dislocation and disconnectedness breed dishonesty. Surveying modern sociological literature,

---

5. Keyes, *The Post-Truth Era,* 32.

6. Immanuel Kant, *Grounding for the Metaphysics of Morals* with "On a Supposed Right to Lie because of Philanthropic Concerns" (Indianapolis: Hackett, 1993). Originally published 1797.

Keyes acknowledges a link between post-truthfulness and the loss of community. "When it comes to post-truthfulness, the fraying of human connections is both cause and effect. Not feeling connected to others makes it easier to lie, which in turn makes it harder to reconnect. Eroded communities foster dishonesty. Dishonesty contributes to the further erosion of communities. As communal bonds wither, unfettered self-interest is unleashed."[7]

Most of us are largely unaware of the pervasive dishonesty around us—even the dishonesty and deception included in our understanding of the past. Keyes goes after several of America's most cherished historical legends, demonstrating that many are "apocryphal in whole or in part." The famous story of George Washington and the cherry tree was invented by a moralistic clergyman, ironically as an argument for honesty.

"Puffery is an art form in the United States," Keyes asserts. Self-invention becomes a way of climbing the social ladder. Ralph Lifshitz transforms himself into Ralph Lauren and spawns one of America's most famous and profitable lifestyle brands. To be sure, the classical and Anglophile style of Ralph Lauren's designs would be more awkwardly marketed under the name Ralph Lifshitz.

Similarly, Keyes identifies Martha Stewart as one of "the quintessential reinvented Americans." Unlike Ralph

---

7. Keyes, *The Post-Truth Era,* 41.

Lauren, who openly acknowledges his origins, Martha Stewart, Keyes accuses, goes to incredible and extreme effort to hide her humble roots. In an article written for an early issue of *Martha Stewart Living*, Stewart wrote an editorial tribute to honesty. "We must remember," she chided, "and teach our children (and perhaps our political figures)—one essential: the truth shall make you free." Nevertheless, Keyes presents a very different picture of America's domestic advisor. "Martha Stewart routinely misrepresented the type of family she grew up in, her father's occupation, whom she dated in college, where her roommate was from, what she earned as a model, the size of party she threw, her husband's ability to father children, how much of her own writing she did, where her home was located (to avoid paying taxes), and why she sold her ImClone stocks."[8]

In the professional world, résumés are now assumed to be inflated. San Francisco mayor Willie Brown once observed, "I don't know anyone who doesn't lie on their résumé." The most pervasive form of "credential inflation" is the listing of unearned degrees. Keyes reports that some half million Americans hold jobs they attained with spurious qualifications, adding that an investigation conducted by the General Accounting Office once revealed twenty-eight senior federal officials who did not actually hold the college degrees they claimed. Hauntingly, Keyes relates that

8.　Keyes, *The Post-Truth Era*, 52–53.

a hospital personnel official told him that job applicants, once informed that their credentials would be checked by a professional firm, sometimes withdrew their applications. Reportedly, nearly a third of those applying for positions took back their applications and never returned.

What about the law? According to *Black's Law Dictionary*, a *legal fiction* is "an assumption that something is true even though it may be untrue." In other words, lawyers are obligated, according to the professional standards of the bar, to use whatever argument will work in defending a client, whether or not it is true. In one perverse case, Keyes documents the work of a Florida prosecutor who argued in court that a pair of teenage boys had killed their father, and then the prosecutor entered another courtroom to argue that a family friend—not the teenagers—was the real murderer.

Making his way through the terrain of deception in American life, Keyes notes that some individuals have become "recreational liars." They spin tales that are willingly received by some as truths. While this may appear harmless, the practice lowers the credibility of the entire society. Lies are now routinely accepted in political argument and in literature. The line between fiction and nonfiction is now blurry at best. Some recent best-selling books in the "nonfiction" category have been highly fictional. Does anyone even care?

Keyes identifies the academic world as the source of much confusion when it comes to honesty. Postmodern philosophers routinely dismiss objective truth and assert that all truth is simply social construction and invention. Authorities in power simply invent truth in order to buttress their authority, the postmodernists allege. Following this logic, lying becomes a means of liberation. As Keyes observes, quoting Jeremy Campbell: "To a postmodernist, being overly concerned with telling the truth 'is a sign of depleted resources, a psychological disorder, a character defect, a kind of linguistic anorexia.'" Debunking the postmodernist worldview, Keyes simply clarifies the obvious: "Asking what constitutes truth is an appropriate topic for intellectual inquiry, but it doesn't follow that the difficulty of identifying what is objectively true gives us license to tell each other lies."[9]

The Post-Truth Era offers perceptive analysis of American culture in the new millennium. Without the recovery of truth, this civilization is doomed to a descent into even deeper levels of deception and dishonesty. As a culture, it's about time we faced the truth about our acceptance of untruthfulness.

9. Keyes, *The Post-Truth Era,* 142, 145.

13

IS ABORTION A MORAL ISSUE?

A Fascinating Debate on the Left

America has been embroiled in a seemingly endless debate over the issue of abortion for nearly five decades now, but the most fascinating dispute on this issue may now be among those who consider themselves to be, in one way or another, advocates of abortion rights.

An unprecedented view into this debate is available on the pages of Slate.com—a popular Web site that features some of the liveliest reporting available anywhere today. This exchange between writers William Saletan and Katha Pollitt did not begin on the Internet but in the pages of the *New York Times* and the *Nation*.

Saletan fired the first salvo, suggesting in an Op-Ed

commentary published in the *New York Times* that pro-choicers should admit that abortion is "bad" and that those who support abortion rights should work toward a truly dramatic reduction in the total number of abortions.[1]

Saletan's argument is not exactly new, either for himself or for the movement he supports. In his 2004 book *Bearing Right: How Conservatives Won the Abortion War,* Saletan offers some of the most incisive and perceptive analysis of the national abortion debate.[2] In essence, Saletan argues that America has settled on a fragile consensus he describes as "conservative pro-choice." Americans are quite squeamish about abortion itself but have resisted efforts to eliminate altogether access to abortion.

Even those who disagree with Saletan must take his argument seriously. Those of us who yearn to see America affirm the sanctity of all human life, born and preborn, must acknowledge that we have much work to do in terms of changing public opinion—the task of reaching the hearts and minds of millions of individual citizens.

That process of reaching hearts and minds is Saletan's concern as well, even as he is a strong defender of abortion

---

1. William Saletan, "Three Decades After Roe, a War We Can All Support," *New York Times,* January 22, 2006, www.nytimes.com/2006/01/22/opinion/22saletan.html?ex=1295586000&en=226e8bcd261f24a5&ei=588&partner=rssnyt&emc=rss.

2. William Saletan, *Bearing Right: How Conservatives Won the Abortion War* (Berkeley and Los Angeles: University of California Press, 2004).

rights. As he sees it, support for abortion rights is diminishing as the pro-life movement has been largely successful in focusing upon the moral status of the fetus and the objectionable—even horrible—nature of abortion itself.

Writing his Op-Ed piece on the thirty-third anniversary of *Roe v. Wade,* Saletan boldly argued: "It's time for the abortion-rights movement to declare war on abortion." That was a rather amazing statement, and Saletan clearly intended to catch the attention of abortion-rights advocates.

"If you support abortion rights, this idea may strike you as nuts," Saletan acknowledged. "But look at your predicament. Most Americans support *Roe* and think women, not the government, should make abortion decisions. Yet they've entrusted Congress and the White House to politicians who oppose legal abortion, and they haven't stopped the confirmations to the Supreme Court of John G. Roberts Jr. and...Samuel A. Alito Jr."

In terms of political analysis, Saletan reminded his pro-choice readers that abortion may have been a "winning issue" for their side sixteen years ago, but no more. "You have a problem," he advised.

His candid analysis was offered so that the pro-abortion movement might awaken from its slumber. "The problem is abortion," he summarized. In order to make his point, he raised the Partial-Birth Abortion Ban Act and the Unborn Victims of Violence Act—both passed overwhelmingly by Congress and signed into law by President Bush—and reminded: "And most Americans supported both bills, because they agree with your opponents about the simplest thing: It's bad to kill a fetus."

Significantly, Saletan then offered his own moral analysis. "They're right. It is bad," he confirmed. "This is why the issue hasn't gone away. Abortion, like race-conscious hiring, generates moral friction. Most people will tolerate it as a lesser evil or a temporary measure, but they'll never fully accept it. They want a world in which it's less necessary. If you grow complacent or try to institutionalize it, they'll run out of patience. That's what happened to affirmative action. And it'll happen to abortion, if you stay hunkered down behind *Roe*."[3] Instead, Saletan argued that the pro-abortion movement should coalesce around an agenda of lowering the total number of abortions and increasing the use of contraceptives.

All this was just too much for Katha Pollitt, a firebrand liberal who serves as a regular columnist for the *Nation*, one of America's most influential journals of liberal opinion. Pollitt was shocked—absolutely *shocked*—that Saletan was ready to speak of abortion in moral terms. This is a move she emphatically rejects. "Inevitably, attacking abortion as a great evil means attacking providers and patients. If abortion is so bad, why not stigmatize the doctors who perform them? Deny the clinic a permit in your town? Make women feel guilty and ashamed for choosing it and make them

---

3. Saletan, "Three Decades After Roe."

sweat so they won't screw up again?" Furthermore, she warned that unwanted pregnancy—and thus the need for an abortion—might soon "join obesity and smoking as unacceptable behavior in polite society."

Taken by itself, this is a truly amazing comment. At the very least, it suggests that, in Katha Pollitt's social circle, obesity and smoking are taken as genuine moral issues, while abortion—the killing of an unborn human—is not.

But there's more. Consider this statement: "The trouble with thinking in terms of zero abortions is that you make abortion so hateful you do the antichoicers' work for them. You accept that the zygote/embryo/fetus has some kind of claim to be born." Did you get that? Any honest reading of her words would lead to the inevitable conclusion that Pollitt believes that the unborn human has *no* "claim to be born."[4]

In Pollitt's view, Saletan was simply giving away the store by admitting that abortion was indeed a serious moral issue and that it is a "bad" reality in and of itself.

From their initial exchange in the *Times* and the *Nation,* Saletan and Pollitt continued their debate at Slate.com.[5] Their exchange took the form of lengthy letters addressed to each other, with Saletan first clarifying what he really intended to say as he argued about abortion in moral terms.

---

4. Katha Pollitt, "Prochoice Puritans," *Nation,* February 13, 2006, www .thenation.com/doc/20060213/pollitt.
5. William Saletan and Katha Pollitt, "Is Abortion Bad?" Slate.com, February 3, 2006, www.slate.com/id/2135209/entry/2135210.

"I'm no fan of the language of sin," he clarified. "But I don't see why we have to shrink from words like good and bad. It's bad to cause a pregnancy in a situation where you're going to end up having an abortion. It's bad to cause a pregnancy in a situation where you can't be a good mom or dad. Our high rates of unintended pregnancy and abortion are a collective moral problem. If we don't want the government to tell us what to do, we'd better address the problem individually."

Beyond this, Saletan also told Pollitt that his purpose was not to create a movement that would combine pro-choicers with the pro-life. Instead, "I'm trying to form a coalition with the public," he suggested.

Saletan is an ardent supporter of abortion rights, but he positions himself in something of a centrist position—at least his position looks somewhat centrist with Katha Pollitt as background. He is concerned that when Pollitt dismisses any claim to life on the part of the fetus, she confuses the fetus with the zygote, "alienating people who see the difference and might support us if they realize we care about it." This is an interesting move, and a move I believe to be destined to fail.

Why? Because Saletan's effort to suggest that the fetus *might* have some claim to life while the zygote evidently does not is based in no clear or compelling scientific definition of life. The human continuum begins with the union of the sperm and the egg and continues throughout gestation and life until natural death. At no point along this continuum does the life suddenly "become" human. Such arguments are based upon convenient abstractions or arbitrarily chosen capacities or characteristics. Pollitt's position is truly abhorrent and radical, but it is at least consistent.

Responding to Saletan, Pollitt accuses him of offering no real rationale for why abortion should be seen as "so outrageous, so terribly morally offensive, so wrong." She is willing to speak of abortion as a "difficult" decision, but that is about all. She explains that opposition to abortion is really an extension of an effort to deny sexual freedom to women and to stigmatize sex outside of marriage. She identifies this with what she sees as the nation's "already broad, deep strain of sexual Puritanism, shame and blame."

Responding to Pollitt, Saletan clarified his position: "This is why I use the word 'bad.' It upsets many people on the left, but for the same reason, it wakes up people in the middle. It's new, and in my opinion, it's true. (I don't use the word 'wrong,' because to me that implies a prohibitive conclusion. 'Bad' is a consideration. Abortion can be a less-bad option than continuing a pregnancy. In that case, it's bad but not wrong.)"

Pollitt remained unmoved. "Morality has to do with rights and duties and obligations between people," she insisted. "So, no: I do not think terminating a pregnancy is wrong. A potential person is not a person, any more than an acorn is an oak tree. I don't think women should have to give birth just because a sperm met an egg. I think women have the right to consult their own wishes, needs, and capacities and produce only loved, wanted children they can care for—or even no children at all. I think we would all be better off as a society if we respected women's ability to make these decisions for themselves and concentrated on caring well for the born. There is certainly enough work there to keep us all very busy."

In the end, Saletan appeared to have retreated somewhat from his argument about the moral status of abortion, but the very fact that he addressed the issue so clearly and candidly is telling in itself. As for Pollitt, she was eventually willing to admit that abortion is "icky" to many people. As she explained this term: "I think that expresses rather well how lots of people feel about abortion: They may not find it immoral or want to see it made illegal, but it disturbs them. It just seems like a bad thing."

Why should pro-lifers pay attention to this debate among advocates of abortion rights? The answer to that question is simple—the exchange between William Saletan and Katha Pollitt demonstrates the inherent weakness of the pro-abortion argument, or its pro-choice variant. Lacking any objective definition of human life and the status of the unborn, the pro-abortion movement is mired in a pattern of endless internal debates and confusions. Saletan's argument is less radical than Pollitt's, but his position is morally arbitrary, based more in pragmatic concern than in moral philosophy.

In any event, the exchange between William Saletan

and Katha Pollitt indicates that the pro-abortion movement knows that it has work to do in reaching the hearts and minds of Americans. The pro-life movement had better remind itself of the same challenge. Both sides are locked in a race to reach the hearts and minds of those still stuck in the middle.

14

WHO'S AFRAID OF THE FETUS?

How America's Abortion Debate Is Changing

The front page of the *New York Times* may well be journalism's most prized piece of real estate. That fact makes the appearance of one particular article all the more surprising and noteworthy. In the paper's February 2, 2005, edition, reporter Neela Banerjee reported on the use of ultrasound technology by crisis-pregnancy centers. In an article headlined "Church Groups Turn to Sonogram to Turn Women from Abortions," Banerjee offered a unique glimpse into one of the most transformative developments in the struggle against abortion.

The article began by introducing Andrea Brown, who at age twenty-four and searching for an abortion provider, came across the Bowie Crofton Pregnancy Center and Medical Clinic in Bowie, Maryland.

When she called the center, Ms. Brown was told that the facility did not perform abortions or provide abortion referrals, but that she could come in for an ultrasound that would ensure the viability of her baby. As Banerjee reported, "When she did, everything changed."

"When I had the sonogram and heard the heartbeat—and for me a heartbeat symbolizes life—after that there was no way I could do it," Ms. Brown recalled. Once she had seen the image of her unborn baby, abortion was no longer an option.[1]

Andrea Brown's testimony is hardly unique. That fact explains why the *New York Times* decided that the emergence of ultrasound technology in the abortion debate is front-page news.

The ultrasound technology now being employed by crisis-pregnancy centers across the country offers unprecedented views into the womb, providing a three-dimensional image of the baby as it develops. At some stages of pregnancy, the images come close to representing a real-time video image of the baby at play, at rest, and in motion. According to the Heidi Group, a Christian organization

---

1. Neela Banerjee, "Church Groups Turn to Sonogram to Turn Women From Abortions," *New York Times*, February 2, 2005. Accessed at www .nytimes.com/2005/02/02/national/02pregnant.html?ex=1183521600& en=a8900be9503e4a01&ei=5070.

that advises crisis-pregnancy centers, up to 90 percent of women visiting the clinics who see their babies through the use of ultrasound technology change their minds and no longer seek an abortion.

Make no mistake—pro-abortion advocates understand what this new development represents. Susanne Martinez, vice president of public policy at the Planned Parenthood Federation of America, told the *New York Times* that the use of such images by pregnancy centers "is coercive." In an amazingly candid statement, Ms. Martinez put the issue in perspective: "From the time they walk into these centers, they are inundated with information that is propaganda and that has one goal in mind. And that is to have women continue with their pregnancies."

Got it? Ms. Martinez clearly believes that something dreadful has happened when women are persuaded to continue with their pregnancies and not seek abortions. Of course, all that makes sense when the Planned Parenthood Federation of America comes into closer view and its real agenda is made clear.

Dr. Sandra M. Christiansen, medical director of the Care Net Pregnancy Center of Frederick, Maryland, countered Martinez's argument: "Women have a right to know what is going on inside their bodies," she insisted, "and we want to provide women with critical information as they face a life-altering procedure and decision. Women will be empowered to choose life." Dr. Christiansen made no effort to hide her motivation. "The motivation is that man and woman are made in God's image, that life is precious."

Nevertheless, Banerjee explained that pro-abortion advocates consider the use of ultrasound to be an unfair pressure tactic. The reporter quoted Nancy Keenan, president of NARAL Pro-Choice America as saying that ultrasounds have medical legitimacy, but they "shouldn't be misused to badger or coerce women by these so-called crisis pregnancy centers."

Of course, the women whose hearts are turned by the experience of seeing their unborn children are not being "coerced" by the pregnancy centers. They are being transformed by the sudden awareness that a living human being resides within their wombs.

As for Andrea Brown—who appeared with her smiling baby in a moving photograph published in the paper's print edition—she intends to practice sexual abstinence until she gets married. Smiling at her daughter, she added, "I have a constant reminder of what can happen if I don't."

The national media have been watching the development of these crisis-pregnancy centers and the impact of ultrasound technology for some time. Writing for the Newhouse News Service, reporter Mark O'Keefe traced the experience of Rebekah Nancarrow, a twenty-three-year-old woman who visited a faith-based pregnancy center in Dallas, Texas. According to O'Keefe's report, Nancarrow went into the clinic almost certain she wanted to undergo an abortion.

Nevertheless, once Nancarrow saw her baby through an ultrasound technology, everything was changed. "She was moving, she was kicking, she had legs." Nancarrow made a promise to her baby on the spot: "I will take care of you."

Susanne Martinez, also cited in O'Keefe's article, charged that the use of ultrasound technology by pregnancy centers "isn't a matter of providing more knowledge, but an attempt to manipulate women." In other words, the abortion industry doesn't want pregnant women to see inside their own wombs—and thus recognize the humanity of their unborn children.[2]

Just how powerful is this new technology? Tom Glessner, president of the National Institute of Family and Life Advocates, headquartered in Fredericksburg, Virginia, argues that the use of ultrasound technology promises to change the entire landscape of abortion in America.

"I'm not a prophet," Glessner told the reporter, "but I do have an educated feel for this thing and the bottom line is this: By the end of this decade, we want to have 1,000 pregnancy centers becoming medical centers with ultrasound." Glessner's hope is that as increasing numbers of women see pictures of their unborn babies, the number of abortions performed will plummet.

---

2. Mark O'Keefe, "Activists Tout Ultrasound Images to Discourage Abortion," Newhouse News Service. Accessed at www.beliefnet.com/story/121/story_12177.htm.

In the Newhouse News Service article, Rebekah Nancarrow recalled that she had first visited Planned Parenthood in 2001 when she discovered she was pregnant. She went because her boyfriend was pressuring her to have an abortion. Nancarrow received an ultrasound test at the Planned Parenthood clinic, she related, but was not allowed to see the results because, as she was told, that would only make the abortion harder on her.

This was just too much for Nancarrow, who then visited the Dallas Pregnancy Resource Center, where she recalls telling the personnel, "I'm only here to give you one shot to get another view on this." That one shot was all it took. Once she saw the image of her living baby, she lost all interest in an abortion. "That sonogram just confirmed 100 percent to me that this was a life within me, not a tissue or a glob."[3]

The panic setting in among the abortion-rights crowd is understandable. Once a woman sees the baby living in her womb, abortion is revealed for what it is—the murder of a living human being. Needless to say, this gets in the way of the abortion-rights agenda and cuts into the profits of the abortion industry. Once the image of the baby is on the screen, the writing is on the wall for the abortionists.

The logic of panic is the only explanation for many

---

3. Mark O'Keefe, "Activists Tout Ultrasound Images to Discourage Abortion."

pro-abortion responses to the use of ultrasound technology. Writing for the *American Prospect,* one of the nation's most liberal political journals, Matthew Nisbet accused General Electric of promoting the pro-life agenda by advertising its new "4D Ultrasound" imaging system. Back in 2002, GE ran a series of television advertisements demonstrating the use of the powerful imaging technology. As Ewan MacColl's ballad "The First Time Ever I Saw Your Face" played in the background, a couple viewed their baby for the first time.[4]

The pro-abortion movement fears the impact of ultrasound technology the way Howard Hughes feared germs. The Web site of the Feminist Women's Health Center, a group that operates abortion clinics in several states, warns women that they should stay away from crisis-pregnancy centers altogether. "Some of these centers offer ultrasound (also known as sonograms). But that does not mean the personnel operating the equipment are medically trained." In truth, most states require a licensed physician to be present as the test is administered, but what the abortion advocates really fear is that the ultrasound technicians *will* be medically trained.

When all else fails, the Feminist Women's Health Center shifts to scare tactics. "If you discover you are seeking

---

4. Matthew Nisbet, "They Bring Good Spin to Life," *American Prospect,* June 14, 2002, http://prospect.org/cs/articles?article=they_bring _good_spin_to_life.

help from an anti-abortion facility, protect yourself from further harassment. Leave the premises immediately and do not return. When you do locate a professional clinic that offers information about all options, be sure to share your… experience with your new counselor so that whatever distortions and misinformation you may have received can be corrected."[5]

There you have it. The abortion-rights movement has finally met its match. The abortion industry is scared to death of the fetus, knowing that the mere image of a living baby in the womb is the refutation of every argument they can assert and all the coercion they would employ.

We stand at the threshold of a transformation in the struggle for life. In time, the impact of this one powerful technology may utterly reshape the abortion debate in America.

As Rebekah Nancarrow came to understand, she was carrying a baby, not a glob of tissue. That vision of life changed everything. Now, the question comes down to this: who's afraid of the fetus?

---

5. "Beware of Anti-Abortion Crisis Pregnancy Centers," Feminist Women's Health Center, www.fwhc.org/abortion/fake.htm.

15

GOD AND THE TSUNAMI

Theology in the Headlines

On December 26, 2004, an earthquake measuring over 9.0 on the Richter scale occurred off the western coast of Sumatra, Indonesia. The quake triggered a series of tsunamis that spread throughout the Indian Ocean and struck coastlines not only in Indonesia and Thailand, near the vicinity of the earthquake, but also thousands of miles away in Sri Lanka, India, and even eastern Africa. By the end of the tragedy, the giant waves had killed some 230,000 people—168,000 in Indonesia alone—and had left millions more homeless and bereaved.

The numbers alone are difficult to take, but the video images are even harder to look at. Satellite pictures taken before and after the massive tsunamis struck unprotected coastlines tell the story. Before the tsunami, a thriving region is clearly visible. In the aftermath, entire towns, villages, and cities have been wiped off the map. A wall of water traveling several hundred miles an hour and reaching the height of a multistory building slammed into Thailand, India, Indonesia, and Sri Lanka with devastating force. At least nine nations were affected, with some of the waves bringing destruction as far away as Somalia on Africa's eastern coast.

The magnitude of this disaster is multiplied when we realize that the very areas most devastated by the tsunamis are among the most impoverished and helpless regions of the earth. On December 26, 2004, families were washed away, children were ripped from their parents' arms, and suffering beyond description settled upon the earth. Why?

That question comes immediately to the mind of any sensitive person and of any individual whose mind is allowed to rest for even a moment upon the magnitude of this disaster. At the first level, the scientific explanation seems clear. A massive earthquake, registering over 9.0 on the Richter scale, occurred deep under the Indian Ocean, just off the western coast of the Indonesian island of Sumatra. In an instant, one of the most beautiful parts of the world became one of the most deadly, as successive mountains of water radiated from the epicenter of the quake and headed for some of the earth's most densely populated coastal areas. The sliding of tectonic plates beneath the surface of the ocean led to massive devastation and a tidal wave of grief and questions.

How do Christians explain this kind of suffering? What do we have to say about the meaning of an event like this? In short order, questions like these found their way to the front pages of the newspapers and the front lines of our cultural conversation. All too soon, confusion was evident, as various religious leaders offered advice and counsel.

Writing in the *Guardian,* reporter Martin Kettle put the problem in clear form: "Earthquakes and the belief in the judgment of God are, indeed, very hard to reconcile. However, no religion that offers an explanation of the world can avoid making some kind of an attempt to fit the two together." Kettle asserted, "As with previous earthquakes, any explanation of this latest one poses us a sharp intellectual choice. Either there is an entirely natural explanation for it, or there is some other kind. Even the natural one is by no means easy to imagine, but it is at least wholly coherent."[1]

For the atheist or agnostic, the natural explanation will suffice. Those who hold to a naturalistic and materialistic worldview will simply see this disaster as one more meaningless event taking place in a meaningless universe. As

---

1. Martin Kettle, "How Can Religious People Explain Something Like This?" *Guardian,* December 28, 2004, www.guardian.co.uk/comment/story/0,,1380094,00.html.

British philosopher Bryan Appleyard concluded, "The simple truth is what it has always been: nature, uncontrolled, unbidden, unpredictable, can still humble our pride and wreck our schemes in an instant. We are a thin film of thought confined to a narrow band around an undistinguished planet orbiting a pretty average star."[2] In other words, this is just one more accident taking place in an accidental world, observed by accidental human creatures.

The challenge to the Christian faith is clear, even as it is often crudely put forth by secular critics. If God is both omnipotent and benevolent, how can disasters like this happen? This question was stated concisely by playwright Archibald MacLeish in his Pulitzer Prize–winning play *J.B.* Through his character Nickles, MacLeish poses the theological challenge: "If God is God, He is not good; if God is good, He is not God."

An example of how not to give a Christian answer was provided by the archbishop of Canterbury, Rowan Williams. Writing in the *Sunday Telegraph,* Williams said: "Every single random, accidental death is something that should upset a faith bound up with comfort and ready answers. Faced with the paralyzing magnitude of a disaster like this, we naturally feel more deeply outraged—and also more deeply helpless. We can't see how this is going to be dealt with, we

---

2. Bryan Appleyard, "Nature in Its Infinite Power Asks an Awkward Question," *Sunday Times* (Sydney), January 2, 2005.

can't see how to make it better. We know, with a rather sick feeling, that we shall have to go on facing it and we can't make it go away or make ourselves feel good."[3] The newspaper headlined the archbishop's column "Of Course This Makes Us Doubt the Existence of God." After the article was published, the archbishop protested the headline, and his spokesman claimed that the paper's characterization of the archbishop's article was "a misrepresentation of the archbishop's views."

In response, the paper acknowledged that while it may have misrepresented the archbishop's argument, nevertheless, "he himself must accept much of the blame." Surely speaking for the paper's readers as well as its editors, the paper observed, "His prose is so obscure, his thought processes so hard to follow, that his message is often unclear." In exasperation, the paper simply concluded, "If Dr. Williams hopes to teach and inspire his flock, he really must learn to express himself more clearly. Otherwise he will be forever doomed to be the victim of his own erudition."[4]

In Australia, much closer to the tragedy, the Anglican dean of Sydney, Phillip Jensen, explained that natural disasters are a part of God's warning that judgment is coming. Jensen was right, of course, as Jesus Himself pointed to

---

3. Rowan Williams, "Of Course This Makes Us Doubt the Existence of God," *Sunday Telegraph,* January 2, 2005, www.telegraph.co.uk/opinion/ main.jhtml?xml=%2Fopinion%2F2005%2F01%2F02%2Fdo0201.xml.

4. Editorial, "Faith in Plain Language," *Daily Telegraph,* January 3, 2005.

natural disasters as a warning to human beings of our own mortality and of the coming judgment of God. Nevertheless, this was too much for more liberal churchmen in Australia. Neil Brown, dean of Saint Mary's Cathedral (Catholic) described Jensen's comments as "a rather horrible belief when you begin to think about it."[5]

Actually, that's orthodox Christian theology when you think about it. Jesus clearly warned His disciples that famines and earthquakes, along with wars and other ominous phenomena, would be the "birth pangs" of coming tribulation and judgment (Matthew 24:7–8).

It is no time for theological hand wringing and evasion when disaster strikes. A great tragedy like this is often the catalyst for bad theology offered as soothing counsel from religious professionals. But a faithful Christian response will affirm the true character and power of God—His omnipotence and His benevolence. God is in control of the entire universe, and there is not even a single atom outside His sovereignty. At the same time, God's goodness and love are beyond question. The Bible leaves no room for equivocation on either truth.

We must speak where the Bible speaks and be silent

---

5. For both Jensen's and Brown's comments, see Lisa Pryor, "God's Will Comments Horrible, Says Dean," *Sydney Morning Herald,* January 3, 2005, www.smh.com.au/news/Asia-Tsunami/Gods-will-comments-horrible-says-dean/2005/01/02/1104601246571.html.

where Scripture is silent. Christians must avoid offering explanations when God has not revealed an explanation. Finally, Christians must respond to a crisis like this by weeping with those who weep, praying with fervent faithfulness, offering concrete assistance in Christ's name, and most importantly, by bearing bold witness to the gospel of Jesus Christ—the only way to bring life out of death.

16

GOD AND THE TSUNAMI

A Christian Response

The tragedy that unfolded in the Indian Ocean in 2004 calls for a clear Christian response. Suggesting that God was simply unable to prevent the tsunamis that destroyed so many lives simply will not do. Nor will blaming the earthquake and tidal waves on fate, or claiming that God sent the destruction as punishment for the victims' sins, or arguing that the tragedy was further proof that God does not exist.

So how are Christians to respond to a tragedy like this? What approach will affirm the full measure of Christian truth while taking the disaster into honest account?

First, a faithful Christian response must affirm the true character and power of God. The Bible leaves no room for doubting either the omnipotence or the benevolence of

God. The God of the Bible is not a passive bystander, nor a deistic Creator who has withdrawn from His creation and is simply watching it unfold. Just as Creation itself was a Trinitarian event, so also the triune God reigns over His creation. There is not one atom or molecule in the entire cosmos that is not under the sovereign rule of God. As the Christian tradition has always affirmed, God's active lordship over the universe is the sole explanation for why the cosmos even holds together.

At the center of this universe is the fundamental fact of the supremacy of Jesus Christ. As the apostle Paul argued in Colossians 1:15–17, "He is the image of the invisible God, the firstborn of all creation. For by Him all things were created, both in the heavens and on earth, visible and invisible, whether thrones or dominions or rulers or authorities—all things have been created through Him and for Him. He is before all things, and in Him all things hold together." Jesus Christ is the explanatory principle of the universe, and any effort to understand the creation apart from its Creator can lead only to confusion.

Liberal theology attempts to solve this problem by cutting God down to size and removing Him from the equation. Having established a truce with the naturalistic worldview, liberal theology simply accommodates itself to the secular temptation by denying God's active and sovereign rule. In other words, God's goodness is affirmed while His greatness is denied. Process theology does this by putting

God within the created order, struggling along with His creation toward maturity. At the popular level, this theological approach was turned into a bestseller in the 1980s by Rabbi Harold Kushner. In his book *When Bad Things Happen to Good People*,[1] the rabbi simply asserts that God is doing the best He can under the circumstances. He would like to prevent tragedies like cancer, hurricanes, and earthquakes from happening, but He is simply unable to do so.

This is not the God who revealed Himself in the Bible. God's omnipotence is clearly revealed and unconditionally asserted. At the same time, God's goodness is equally affirmed. Christians must point to these conjoined truths as the very basis for our confidence that life is worth living and that God is ultimately in control of the universe.

Second, we must avoid attempting to explain what God has not explained. In the end, the Christian knows that all suffering—indeed every experience of life—is meaningful. We understand that God is revealing Himself in every moment of our existence. We also know that all suffering is ultimately caused by sin. That's about as politically incorrect an assertion as we can now imagine—but it is profoundly true. Even so, we must be very careful in how we present this truth. In the gospel of John (John 9:1–7), Jesus and His disciples were confronted with a man blind from birth. His

---

1. Harold S. Kushner, *When Bad Things Happen to Good People* (New York: Schoken, 1981).

disciples, posing the conventional question of their day, asked Jesus: "Rabbi, who sinned, this man or his parents, that he would be born blind?" (verse 2). Jesus responded that it was neither the sin of this man nor the sin of his parents that explained his blindness; rather, "it was so that the works of God might be displayed in him" (verse 3). In other words, Jesus boldly explained that this man was born blind so that in the miracle Jesus was about to perform, his restored sight would be evidence of the dawning of the kingdom and of the glory of God.

Armed with this knowledge, we must be very circumspect in assigning blame for natural evil. Were the people of Indonesia, Thailand, Sri Lanka, and India more sinful than all others? Did God send this tsunami because of the paganisms so prevalent in South and Southeast Asia? Martin Kettle posed an interesting observation: "Certainly the giant waves generated by the quake made no attempt to differentiate between the religions of those whom it made its victims. Hindus were swept away in India, Muslims were carried off in Indonesia, Buddhists in Thailand. Visiting Christians and Jews received no special treatment either."[2]

We are in absolutely no position to argue that there is no link between human sin and this awful tragedy. The

---

2. Martin Kettle, "How Can Religious People Explain Something Like This?" *Guardian,* December 28, 2004, www.guardian.co.uk/comment/story/0,,1380094,00.html.

Bible makes clear that God sometimes does respond to specific sin with cataclysmic natural disaster. Just ask the towns of Sodom and Gomorrah. Nevertheless, in the book of the Bible most centrally concerned with the issue of suffering, it is Job's friends who tried to offer detailed theological explanations and ended up looking foolish—and worse. Job himself was censured by God for "darken[ed] counsel by words without knowledge" (Job 38:2). In the end, Job is vindicated by God's grace and mercy, and Job can only respond, "I know that You can do all things, and that no purpose of Yours can be thwarted. 'Who is this that hides counsel without knowledge?' Therefore I have declared that which I did not understand, things too wonderful for me, which I did not know.... I have heard of You by the hearing of the ear; but now my eye sees You; therefore I retract, and I repent in dust and ashes" (Job 42:1–3, 5–6). Job's humility should serve as a model for our own.

As the apostle Paul reminds us, the judgments of God are "unsearchable" and "unfathomable" (Romans 11:33). Unless God reveals the purpose of His acts and the working of His will among us, we would do well to affirm His sovereignty and goodness, while holding back from placing blame on human agents for disasters such as earthquakes and hurricanes.

At the same time, the Bible is clear that sin is the fundamental explanation for these awful disasters. Not sin that is immediately traceable to one individual or another, or even to a specific culture, but the sin that is so clearly indicted in the biblical account of the Fall. According to Genesis 3, Adam's sin had cosmic implications and effects. The effects of sin are evident all around us, most clearly in the undeniable fact of death. This is why the redemptive work of God in Christ points to a new heaven and a new earth as coming realities. As Paul explains, "We know that the whole creation groans and suffers the pains of childbirth together until now" (Romans 8:22). In Revelation 21, we are told of a new heaven and a new earth and of a day when God will wipe away every tear from the eyes of the redeemed, "and there will no longer be any death; there will no longer be any mourning, or crying, or pain; the first things have passed away" (verse 4).

Third, Christians must respond with the love of Christ and the power of the gospel. Jesus is our great example in responding to such crises. When confronted with the man born blind, Jesus healed the man and showed the glory of God. In response to the death of Lazarus, Jesus brought life out of death, even as He had mourned with Lazarus's sisters.

While Christians are not empowered to perform similar miracles, we are called to be agents of Christ's love and mercy. Following our Lord's example, we must first mourn with those who mourn. The unspeakable grief and incalculable suffering experienced by literally millions of persons in South and Southeast Asia should prompt every believer in the Lord Jesus Christ to fervent prayer, concern, generosity, and sympathy.

Moreover, Christians should be at the forefront of relief efforts. In the days and months after the tsunami, churches, denominations, and Christian agencies sent support in the form of food, medical care, reconstruction programs, and other forms of humanitarian assistance. In offering concrete help and assistance, Christians were doing nothing less than following the express command and example of Jesus Christ.

Beyond this, Christians must seize opportunities to confront natural disasters with the life-changing power of the gospel of Jesus Christ. Christians are to feed the hungry, give drink to the thirsty, and clothe the naked in the name of Christ. This is a powerful testimony, but acts of compassion must be accompanied by words of conviction. Our answer to the reality of unspeakable tragedy must be to witness to the gospel of unfathomable power—the power to bring life out of death.

Furthermore, we must indeed point to natural disasters as only a hint of the cataclysm that is yet to come—the holy judgment of God. On that day, the tidal waves of December 26, 2004, will be understood to have been one of the warnings all humanity should have heeded.

This is no time for Christian equivocation or cowardice. In the face of tragedy and suffering on this scale, we must answer with the full measure of Christian conviction and the undiluted truth of Christianity. In this life, we are not given all the answers to the questions we might pose, but God has given us all that we need to know in order to understand our peril and His provision for us in Christ. So let us weep with those who weep, pray for those who suffer, give and go in missions of mercy, and bear bold witness to the gospel of Jesus Christ.

17

NINEVEH, NEW ORLEANS, AND THE CITY OF MAN

An Eternal Perspective

C ities do not last. Those built in precarious places collapse. The rest are doomed to decay or suffer humanly induced destruction." That is the assessment of historian Felipe Fernández-Armesto.[1] He spoke those words with reference to New Orleans in the aftermath of Hurricane Katrina, but his historical judgment would well apply to Nineveh, Tyre, Babylon, and a host of cities long ago covered with dust.

---

1. Felipe Fernández-Armesto, "From Nineveh to New Orleans," *Times* (London), September 10, 2005.

The pictures that came out of New Orleans in 2005 tell the story. Broken glass, twisted steel, sunken streets, and abandoned homes testified of the city's impermanence. Yet the pictures of devastation wrought by nature paled against the picture of moral devastation that followed the hurricane. Lawlessness in the streets, rioting in the Superdome, and sniper fire aimed at rescue teams revealed the disorder and anarchy that lie close beneath the surface of human civilization.

Of all people, Christians should be least surprised. After all, we have been warned of civilization's fragility, and we know that history unfolds God's judgment in the rising and falling of empires, nations, and cities. Augustine, the great theologian-bishop of Hippo in North Africa, produced the greatest interpretation of history by a Christian in his monumental work *The City of God*. Writing even as Rome had fallen to the Vandals, Augustine offered a Christian vision of history and its meaning.

Christians should see all of history in terms of two cities, Augustine explained—an earthly city and a heavenly city. The earthly city, the City of Man, serves the gods of power, wealth, and pleasure. Its ultimate founder is Cain, who, according to Genesis 4:17, "built a city." Cain's city, and all the lesser cities that follow in its way, are transient monuments to human achievement and pride. Christians are indeed citizens of the earthly city, Augustine argued. But as the New Testament makes clear, we are ultimately citizens of a heavenly kingdom—the City of God. As Augustine wrote, "We have learnt that there is a City of God: and we have longed to become citizens of that City with a love inspired by its founder."[2]

Augustine understood that the two cities represented two different allegiances, two different loves, and two different ways of life. Ultimately, the two cities represent two very different destinies. The earthly city is concerned with the matters that make for glory and pleasure among men. The City of God, embodied in this age as the church, is the eternal city that is completely devoted to the glory of God. The earthly city is headed for destruction. The City of God is eternal.

The earthly city looks secure but is passing. This truth is brought to mind when looking at the remains of New Orleans. Buildings that once looked so permanent and safe have been demolished and replaced. Institutions and organizational forms that once constituted the very structure of civilization can quickly pass from existence. Anarchy quickly supplants order, and ruins quickly appear where gardens had once been tended.

"The ruins of places once full of confidence surround

---

2. Augustine, *The City of God Against the Pagans*, Cambridge Texts in the History of Political Thought, (Cambridge: Cambridge University Press, 1998).

us," reminds Fernández-Armesto. "History is a path we pick among them. Yet we contemplate them with romantic yearning or philosophical detachment, instead of being very afraid."[3]

Of course, Fernández-Armesto is right. Fear would be an appropriate response to what we saw in New Orleans after the hurricane. As Augustine reminds us, "The earthly city will not be everlasting; for when it is condemned to the final punishment it will no longer be a city. It has its good in this world, and rejoices to participate in it with such gladness as can be derived from things of such a kind. And since this is not the kind of good that causes no frustrations to those enamoured of it, the earthly city is generally divided against itself by litigation, by wars, by battles, by the pursuit of victories that bring death with them, or at best are doomed to death."[4]

Cities appear to be permanent, but no city has endured throughout the course of human history. No earthly city will endure the judgment that is to come.

Fernández-Armesto sympathizes with our reflexive trust in cities.

The fragility of cities is a cruel fact to acknowledge.

We put so much effort into them. We beautify them

---

3. Fernández-Armesto, "From Nineveh to New Orleans."

4. Augustine, *The City of God.*

in confidence of the future. We measure their greatness by their willingness to make present sacrifices
for future fame, or—more altruistically—for the
benefit of posterity. We admire cities that court disaster. Dazzlingly heroic examples include Venice—
built in stone on islets of salt marsh, so that it is
bound to sink; or San Francisco, built and rebuilt in
defiance of topography and almost in the embrace
of a geological fault-line; or Tokyo, earthquake
prone and in the path of typhoons.[5]

Even a brief review of human history tells the story.
Augustine wrote *The City of God* as a Christian interpretation of history that had been made necessary by the fall of
Rome. When the Visigoths plundered Rome in AD 410
(followed by the Ostrogoths in 455), the capital city of the
Roman Empire fell—and the fall of that city was indeed
great. By the end of the fifth century, only a hundred thousand citizens lived in Rome, the rich having fled to Con-
stantinople or other safe and attractive cities. The capital
that had styled itself the Eternal City was now a desolate
ruin. Christopher Woodward recalls, "In the sixth century
the Byzantines and the Goths contested the city three times,
and the population fell to thirty thousand clustered in
poverty beside the River Tiber, now that the aqueducts had

---

5. Fernández-Armesto, "From Nineveh to New Orleans."

been destroyed and the drinking fountains were dry. The fall of Rome came to be seen by many as the greatest catastrophe in the history of western civilization."[6]

Poetry and literature are filled with references to ruins and the passing of civilization. Percy Bysshe Shelley told the story of King Ozymandius, whose abandoned statue mocked his claim to be "Ozymandius, king of kings." As Shelley described the scene: "Nothing beside remains, round the decay / of that colossal wreck, boundless and bare / the lone and level sands stretch far away."[7] Standing at the very apex of Queen Victoria's empire, Rudyard Kipling warned of the judgment that was to come. "Far-call'd our navies melt away / on dune and headland sinks the fire. / Lo, all our pomp of yesterday / is one with Nineveh and Tyre!" he intoned.[8]

Remember that Augustine described the two cities as created by two kinds of love. As he taught his fellow Christians, "The earthly city was created by self-love reaching the contempt of God, the heavenly city by the love of God carried as far as contempt of self. In fact, the earthly city glories in itself, the heavenly city glories in the Lord. The former looks for glory from men, the latter finds its highest glory in God, the witness of a good conscience."[9] Alas, we are

6. Christopher Woodward, *In Ruins* (New York: Pantheon, 2002).

7. Percy Bysshe Shelley, *Ozymandius* (1818).

8. Rudyard Kipling, *Recessional* (1897).

9. Augustine, *The City of God*.

tempted by the wrong love, and we are easily seduced by the wrong city.

Augustine was absolutely certain—and absolutely correct—in emphasizing the temporary nature of the earthly city and the passing power of its love. Only the heavenly city remains, and all earthly cities will follow Nineveh, Tyre, Babylon, and every other metropolis and village into oblivion. One day, unless that Day of Judgment comes sooner, New Orleans, New York, San Francisco, and all the cities we now know and admire will be covered with dust, if not with water.

In the midst of all this, the church—representing the City of God—must keep its wits about it. Jerome, one of the great leaders of the church as Rome fell, asked the wrong question: "What is to become of the church now that Rome has fallen?" The City of God is represented wherever the church is found, and the church is safe by the power of God. Christians must be humbled by a biblical view of history that understands the difference between the earthly and the heavenly cities, one that understands full well that every earthly city will fall and that only the City of God will remain. In the meantime, we should pray humble prayers and ask for God to preserve the earthly city until His kingdom comes. As Kipling called England to pray: "Lord God of Hosts be with us yet, lest we forget, lest we forget!"[10]

---

10. Kipling, *Recessional.*

18

HIROSHIMA AND THE BURDEN OF HISTORY

A Transforming Event

S timson, what was gunpowder? Trivial. What was electricity? Meaningless. This atomic bomb is the second coming in wrath!" Those words were spoken by British prime minister Winston Churchill to U.S. secretary of war Henry Stimson. The two men were gathered at the Potsdam Conference in July 1945, and Churchill had just been informed that America had successfully tested an atomic bomb.[1]

---

1. Herbert Feis, *Japan Subdued: The Atomic Bomb and the End of the War in the Pacific* (Princeton, NJ: Princeton University Press, 1961), 72–73, 75.

In one sense, human history was transformed the moment that bomb exploded in the New Mexico desert, but it was the first use of an atomic bomb in warfare that is seared into human memory. On August 6, 1945, Col. Paul Tibbets and his crew flew the *Enola Gay*, their specially modified B-29 bomber, and dropped "Little Boy" over the city of Hiroshima, Japan.

The power and destructive force of the bomb defied human imagination, and it continues to do so today. Within seconds of its detonation, the bomb had destroyed most of central Hiroshima. A giant fireball unleashed annihilation and a consuming inferno throughout the city. Buildings, bridges, and human bodies were vaporized by the force of the blast as successive shockwaves spread across the region and a now-familiar mushroom cloud reached heights of over forty-eight thousand feet above the city. Just three days later, an even more destructive bomb would be dropped over the city of Nagasaki.

News of the bomb and its power soon spread around the world. Joseph Stalin had been informed of the American development of the bomb during the Potsdam Conference in the summer of 1945. According to historians, he then went into an entire day of mourning and seclusion. The actual use of the bomb could not be hidden from the human consciousness. Indeed, the American use of the bomb was intended to break the Japanese military's will to fight.

At first, the American people responded to news of the bomb with a sense of relief. This was especially true for millions of American soldiers, who knew that the alternative to a Japanese surrender was a ghastly invasion of the Japanese mainland. Just after dropping the bomb, navigator Theodore "Dutch" Van Kirk heard someone aboard the *Enola Gay* express, "This war is over." As Van Kirk later reflected, he silently agreed with the assessment. "You didn't see how anybody—even the most radical, militaristic, uncaring for their people—how anybody like that could stand up to something like this."[2] Writer Paul Fussell, a twenty-one-year-old soldier serving in France and waiting for likely deployment for the Japanese invasion, expressed his thoughts with simple relief: "We were going to live. We were going to grow up to adulthood after all."[3]

The actual destruction wrought by the bomb was classically described by novelist John Hersey in *Hiroshima* in 1946.[4] Much of the book had already appeared in a series of articles Hersey wrote for the *New Yorker*. The human toll eventually numbered somewhere between 100,000 and

2. "Theodore 'Dutch' Van Kirk, 84," *Time*, July 23, 2005, www.time .com/time/world/article/0,8599,1086088,00.html. A shorter version of the article appeared in the August 1, 2005, edition of *Time*.

3. Michael Elliott, "Living Under the Cloud," *Time*, August 1, 2005, www.time.com/time/magazine/article/0,9171,1086168,00.html.

4. John Hersey, *Hiroshima* (New York: Knopf, 1946).

200,000 deaths. An estimated 120,000 were killed immediately in Hiroshima and Nagasaki, but thousands of others died later from catastrophic injuries and the effects of radiation.

In the years since the Japanese surrender, the American use of atomic weapons at Hiroshima and Nagasaki has become one of the most debated questions of history. The burden of history falls upon all of us, but Christians bear a particular responsibility to make sense of the past and to evaluate events, issues, and decisions from the framework of Christian moral teaching. For some, a quick condemnation of nuclear weapons is the only conceivable response. Those who hold to such a position of absolute condemnation assume that President Harry S. Truman and his colleagues were war criminals. On the other hand, the majority of Americans living at the time saw the use of the weapon as beyond question, believing it to have been necessary in order to force a Japanese surrender and to prevent an even greater death toll in Japanese and American lives.

When the Smithsonian Institution decided to create a special exhibit focused on the *Enola Gay* and its mission on the fiftieth anniversary of the Hiroshima bombing in 1995, a contentious controversy and battle among historians ensued. As Richard B. Frank explains, the "traditionalist" view held by historians understands that the United States had used the two atomic bombs in order to end the war in the

Pacific. "They further believed that those bombs had actually ended the war and saved countless lives," Frank explains.[5]

In contrast, historical "revisionists" argue that the use of the atomic weapon was actually motivated by the American concern that the Soviet Union might gain advantage in the Pacific. According to the revisionists, the Japanese were already attempting to surrender, but Truman dropped the bomb in order to prevent the Soviets from claiming more territory in the Pacific. Nevertheless, there is no evidence that the Japanese were really ready to surrender—certainly not on the unconditional terms of the Potsdam Declaration. In reality, the Japanese were engaged in a high-stakes gamble that the Soviets would force the Americans and the British to negotiate.

Frank offers a compelling argument that the revisionists are simply wrong. In an article published in the August 8, 2005, issue of the *Weekly Standard,* Frank argues that new evidence, mostly drawn from declassified intelligence reports, demonstrates that the Japanese high command was not even close to a decision to surrender and that the Allied demand for a Japanese unconditional surrender was still

---

5. Richard B. Frank, "Why Truman Dropped the Bomb," *Weekly Standard,* August 8, 2005, www.weeklystandard.com/Content/Public/Articles/000/000/005/894mnyyl.asp.

rejected by Japanese authorities. As a decoded message from Foreign Minister Shigenori Togo stated to his ambassador to Russia: "Please bear particularly in mind, however, that we are not seeking the Russians' mediation for anything like an unconditional surrender."

More than six decades later, it is now clear that the developing cold war between the United States and the Soviet Union did play a part in the background to the conclusion of the Pacific war. Nevertheless, we also now know that the Japanese war council was adamantly opposed to surrender, even as defeat was virtually certain. A decision to surrender—with the understanding that the Japanese monarchy would survive in revised form—came only after Emperor Hirohito personally intervened to force the issue.

In his brilliant and controversial new book *Racing the Enemy: Stalin, Truman, and the Surrender of Japan,* historian Tsuyoshi Hasegawa of the University of California, Santa Barbara, argues, "The Japanese leaders knew that Japan was losing the war. But defeat and surrender are not synonymous. Surrender is a political act. Without the twin shocks of the atomic bombs and Soviet entry into the war, the Japanese would never have accepted surrender in August."[6] Hasegawa argues that it was the combination of the two atomic bombs and the Soviet declaration of war on

---

6. Tsuyoshi Hasegawa, *Racing the Enemy: Stalin, Truman, and the Surrender of Japan* (Cambridge, MA: Belknap Press of Harvard University Press, 2005).

August 8 that led to a collapse in the Japanese war party. Nevertheless, we should remember that an attempted coup against the emperor and the government was almost successful, even as Hirohito prepared to announce the surrender to his nation.

Decades after the event, we know much more about the sequence of events that shaped the context and about the deliberations that shaped the decisions on both the Japanese and American sides. Writing in the August 1, 2005, edition of *Time* magazine, Michael Elliott summarizes: "Ever since, there has been controversy over when the war would have ended had the bomb not been dropped on Hiroshima…and how many Japanese and Americans would have died before it did. But, plainly, the most terrible war ever known ended earlier than it would have because of the *Enola Gay*'s mission. The bombs cost tens of thousands of lives…but they saved lives too." Elliott adds, "Right from the start, the nuclear age was wrapped in a paradox. An awful weapon had saved lives; a terrible instrument of war had brought peace."[7]

Was the use of the atomic bomb categorically wrong? Some are certain that it was. Nevertheless, catastrophic bombing of populations had already taken place in both the Pacific and European theaters of the war. As Jerram Barrs, of Covenant Seminary in St. Louis argues, nuclear weapons

---

7. Elliott, "Living Under the Cloud."

"are qualitatively different, capable of greater destruction than conventional weapons, but not of a quite different order." As he explains: "Man has shown, again and again, that he can kill millions of people with quite simple weapons (Julius Caesar's wars in Gall are one example). The ability to kill many with one bomb is not qualitatively different from killing many with swords or guns."[8]

The most challenging moral questions related to the use of the bomb in Hiroshima and Nagasaki are whether the bomb was actually necessary to end the war and whether it was right to bomb cities, knowing that thousands of civilians would be among the casualties. Here again, Barrs argues that "while the desire to keep civilians out of battle is obviously praiseworthy, we have to recognize that this is sometimes difficult." When military assets are deeply embedded within civilian populations, the issue becomes even more troubling.

The Christian conscience must continue to struggle with the morality of the atomic age and with the specter of nuclear weapons. We must be thankful that sixty years have now passed without any further hostile use of nuclear weaponry. Whatever moral questions may be addressed to

---

8. Jerram Barrs, "The Just War Revisted," *Pacifism and War: Eight Prominent Christians Debate Today's Issues,* ed. Oliver R. Barclay (Leicester, UK: InterVarsity, 1984), 157.

the cold war doctrine of Mutual Assured Destruction, the fact is that neither the Soviet Union nor the United States used a nuclear weapon against the other. The current picture is further complicated by the fact that the proliferation of nuclear weapons remains a paramount concern. Most contemporary observers believe that the greatest danger posed by a nuclear weapon is that one might be used by a terrorist group.

In the final analysis, there is good reason to believe that the deployment of the atomic bombs in Hiroshima and Nagasaki may well have saved more Japanese lives in the end, as well as the lives of unnumbered American soldiers and sailors.

I cannot reflect on this question without thinking of my friend Joe Reynolds, who was then a young marine officer who had seen the carnage of Iwo Jima firsthand. Had Japan not surrendered in August 1945, Joe Reynolds and millions of other American servicemen would have invaded Japan, facing a nation then willing to fight the invaders to the bitter end—even if it meant elderly women and young children wielding sharpened bamboo spears. I am thankful that that tragic war did end in August 1945, and I am thankful that Joe Reynolds, along with millions of his fellow soldiers and sailors, lived to serve their country in other ways.

The sobering memory of the Hiroshima bombing should serve as a catalyst for Christian reflection on the morality of warfare, the reality of human sinfulness, the frailty of human wisdom, and the burden of history. For all these things, we will give an answer. Until then, we must do the very best with what we have, what we know, and what we face.

19

THE CONTENT OF OUR CHARACTER

King's Dream and Ours

I have a dream," declared Dr. Martin Luther King Jr., as he addressed a crowd of several hundred thousand gathered on the Mall in Washington, D.C. The date was August 28, 1963, and America was a cauldron of social unrest.

Civil rights leaders had called for the March on Washington in order to force the nation to deal with the so-called race problem. As the event drew to a close, all eyes were on the final speaker. The crowd standing in Washington's sweltering heat waited for the man they knew would be the closer of the event. Most Americans recognized the name, face, and voice of Martin Luther King Jr. He had appeared on the nation's front pages and news broadcasts, having led major protests and movements in Montgomery and Birmingham, Alabama, and other cities. And yet King was an enigma to many white Americans. What would he say?

Interestingly, the most famous words of his speech were not included in his manuscript. King had arrived in Washington the day before and had prepared his speech in a room at the famous Willard Hotel. In *The Dream: Martin Luther King, Jr., and the Speech That Inspired a Nation,* author Drew D. Hansen provides a parallel text of Dr. King's manuscript and his actual words.[1] When he reached the pinnacle of his oratory, King simply departed from his prepared text and launched his speech into history.

"I say to you today, my friends, so even though we face the difficulties of today and tomorrow, I still have a dream. It is a dream deeply rooted in the American dream." Dr. King spoke of a dream "that one day on the red hills of Georgia, the sons of former slaves and the sons of former slave owners will be able to sit down together at the table of brotherhood." More personally, "I have a dream that my four little children will one day live in a nation where they will not be judged by the color of their skin but by the content of their character. I have a dream today."

In the midst of a nation torn by racial strife and social unrest, Dr. King painted an indelible picture of America as

---

1. Drew D. Hansen, *The Dream: Martin Luther King, Jr., and the Speech That Inspired a Nation* (New York: HarperCollins, 2005).

it could be and should be. His oratory was soaring, his imagery was vivid, and his cause was right. His cadences, inflections, and biblical allusions gave the speech its memorable structure. His powerful argument gave the speech its moral weight. The speech is as much a part of our national memory as Abraham Lincoln's Gettysburg Address. Speaking to a generation poised to reject the American dream as a lie, Dr. King challenged them to make it their own. He rejected claims that America could never be reformed or called to its moral senses.

We do well to look back to 1963 and remember the reality. In the South, Jim Crow laws enforced segregation. Separate motels, restaurants, schools, and water fountains marked the moral landscape. In the North, the absence of Jim Crow laws did not mean that the races were integrated. North and South, black and white Americans inhabited different worlds. African Americans were routinely denied access to accommodations, higher education, and the voting booth.

Those standing on the nation's mall that day could not have known that years of struggle, frustration, violence, and tragedy lay ahead. Observing America in 1835, Alexis de Tocqueville wrote, "I do not imagine that the white and black race will ever live in any country upon an equal footing. But I believe the difficulty to be still greater in the United States than elsewhere." His words proved an understatement. Obstructionists attempted to block racial progress at every turn. Some white Americans just could not abide the idea of racial equality and full integration. On the other hand, Stanford University professor Shelby Steele traces how many of the civil rights leaders traded moral consciousness for racial consciousness and abandoned the vision of racial equality for identity politics.

Still, America is a very different nation now. Racial discrimination is prohibited by law. Statements of prejudice are now socially unthinkable and politically incorrect. Black America can now claim many in positions of influence and leadership in all spheres of public life. Poverty still holds many in its grip, but the majority of African Americans are in the middle class. Nevertheless, much ground remains to be recovered.

Southern conservatives bear a special burden, especially as Christians. I was not yet four years old on August 28, 1963. I have no memory of hearing Dr. King deliver his famous address. A white boy raised in the South, I had not seen any black persons at close hand. I had seen black workers, field hands, and children, but all at a distance. I had no black friends and no black neighbors and saw no black faces at school or at church. To the best of my knowledge, I attended segregated schools until the fifth grade. Later, living in a major metropolitan area, I attended integrated middle and high schools with hundreds of black students. I came to know black teenagers at school, work, Boy Scouts, and other activities. I considered several of them to be friends, but I never really entered their lives. It now dawns on me that I have no idea where they may be living or what they may be doing.

Now I know many African Americans as cherished friends and treasured colleagues. I cannot imagine a world in which this is not normal, nor can our children. But honesty compels me to admit that this is more because my black friends have entered my world than that I have entered theirs.

Christians must begin with the affirmation that all human beings are equally created in the image of God. But we also realize that we are sinners, and sin is the fundamental problem on the issue of race. Sin is so interwoven in our lives and institutional structures that we often cannot even see it. The only real remedy for the problem of racial prejudice is the transforming power of the Lord Jesus Christ. His atonement for sin is the only cure, and the only real picture of true racial reconciliation is that found in Revelation 7:9–12, where we read of the redeemed people of God as "a great multitude which no one could count, from every nation and all tribes and peoples and tongues, standing before the throne and before the Lamb." The Lamb will make us one.

There is much work to do. We struggle in a fallen world until Jesus comes. By God's grace, we know that real progress is possible and that we are accountable. The church must show the world that the new community of Jesus is called to demonstrate His glory in calling us together.

The Christian doctrine of humanity revealed in the Bible is the only adequate foundation for dealing with racism. Ultimately, we really *do* believe that every single human being is made in the image of God and reflects God's glory by his or her very existence. We believe that God delights in the racial and ethnic diversity of those made in His image—or we simply refuse to believe what the Bible so clearly teaches us.

20

THE CHALLENGE
OF ISLAM

A Christian Perspective

President Barack Obama has put the issue of Islam front and center on the international stage. His visit to Turkey in 2009, and his very public statements to the Muslim world, have raised a host of questions at home and abroad.

In his speech to the Turkish parliament, President Obama declared, "The United States is not, and never will be, at war with Islam." He went on to say that "our partnership with the Muslim world is critical not just in rolling back the violent ideologies that people of all faiths reject, but also to strengthen opportunity for all its people."

But the president also spoke of his "deep appreciation for the Islamic faith." Here is the statement in context:

I also want to be clear that America's relationship with the Muslim community, the Muslim world, cannot, and will not, just be based upon opposition to terrorism. We seek broader engagement based on mutual interest and mutual respect. We will listen carefully, we will bridge misunderstandings, and we will seek common ground. We will be respectful, even when we do not agree. We will convey our deep appreciation for the Islamic faith, which has done so much over the centuries to shape the world—including in my own country. The United States has been enriched by Muslim Americans. Many other Americans have Muslims in their families or have lived in a Muslim-majority country—I know, because I am one of them.

At a press conference in Turkey, the president made yet another statement:

One of the great strengths of the United States is…we have a very large Christian population—we do not consider ourselves a Christian nation or a Jewish nation or a Muslim nation. We consider ourselves a nation of citizens who are bound by ideals and a set of values.

On CNN, with host Roland Martin, the same day that President Obama spoke in Turkey, I said,

I think President Obama rightly said that the United
States is not at war with Islam—I think that is a
very helpful clarification.

But you can't take Islam out of the whole civilizational struggle we are in, not only in the war on
terror, but frankly, going back for centuries, coming
up with a definition of what a good civilization
would look like and how a society ought to be
arranged.

I do think President Obama was correct in stating that
the United States is not at war with Islam. This is important
not only in terms of international diplomacy but also in
terms of constitutional authority. The government of the
United States has no right or authority to declare war on any
religion.

Yet at the same time we need to understand the political
context: the president was in Turkey. Given the confusion
rampant in the Muslim world, that is a crucial clarification.
Of course, a quick review of the statements of President
George W. Bush reveal that he said much the same thing,
over and over again.

The fact that President Obama made these comments
in Turkey is very important. Throughout the Muslim world,
most Muslims *do* see the United States as being at war with
Islam. Classical Islam understands no real distinction between religion and the state but instead establishes a unitary

society. Thus, when a foreign power like the United States invades a Muslim nation like Iraq, most Muslims see this as a war against Islam.

While specific forms of government vary in the Islamic world, this general understanding holds true. Unlike New Testament Christianity, Islam is essentially a territorial religion including all lands under submission to the rule of the Qur'an. The President was in Turkey when he made these statements, and Turkey is usually defined in the media as having a secular government. Indeed, the Turkish constitution even requires a secular government. But, as anyone who visits Turkey quickly discovers, *secular* has a very unusual definition.

Being Muslim is part of what the Turkish people and government call Turkishness, a unifying concept that goes all the way back to Mustafa Kemal Atatürk, the founder of modern Turkey. Offending Turkishness is a criminal act in Turkey. The Turkish government is the steward of every one of the seemingly countless mosques within the nation, and it pays the imams. Turkey may be considered a Muslim nation with a secular government, but its secular character would not be seen as anything close to secular from an American perspective.

In this light, President Obama's statement that America is not a Christian country is accurate and helpful, though he was criticized by many conservative Christians for making the claim. His clarification, offered in Muslim Turkey, established as a matter of public fact the reality that our American constitutional system is very different from what is found in the Muslim world—and even in Turkey itself.

Furthermore, if the United States is to be understood as a Christian nation in the same sense that most nations in the Islamic world consider themselves to be Muslim nations, then America *is* at war with Islam.

The controversy over the president's remarks in this context are thus misplaced. There is indeed a controversy over whether it is appropriate to call America a Christian nation in the sense that Americans would even make such a claim—but the context in Turkey and the Muslim world is very different. Do American Christians really believe that Christianity benefits by being associated with all that America represents in the Muslim world? To many Muslims, America appears as the great fountain of pornography, debased entertainments, abortion, and sexual revolution. Does it help our witness to Christ that all this would be associated in the Muslim mind with "Christian" America?

Beyond any historical doubt, the United States was established by founders whose worldview was shaped, in most cases quite consciously, by the Christian faith. The founding principles of this nation flow from a biblical logic and have been sustained by the fact that most Americans have considered themselves Christians and have operated out of a Christian frame of moral reference. America is a nation whose citizens are overwhelmingly identified as Christians, and the American experiment is inconceivable without the foundation established by Christian moral assumptions.

But America is not, by definition, a Christian nation in any helpful sense. The secularists and enemies of the faith make this argument for any number of hostile and antagonistic reasons, and they offer many false arguments as well. But this should not prompt American Christians to make bad arguments of our own.

I criticized President Obama not for stating that America is not at war with Islam but for failing to be honest in clarifying that we do face a great civilizational challenge in Islam. Islam is the single most vital competitor to Western ideals of civilization on the world scene. The logic of Islam is to bring every square inch of this planet under submission to the rule of the Qur'an. Classical Islam divides the world into the World of Islam and the World of War. In this latter world the struggle to bring society under submission to the Qur'an is still ongoing.

President Obama created his own confusion over these issues, subverting his main point. If America is not at war with Islam, it seems unhelpful for the Obama administration to now refer to Iran, against previous American practice, as the Islamic Republic of Iran. Similarly, some of President Obama's words and gestures during his trip seemed overly indulgent toward Islam—especially pertaining to the way these words and gestures would have been interpreted in the larger Islamic world.

Submission of the whole world to the Qur'an is the ambition that drives the Muslim world—and each faithful Muslim. They hope, pray, and work toward this purpose. Most Muslims are not willing to employ terrorism in order to achieve this goal. Nevertheless, it remains the goal.

Islam and the West offer two very different and fundamentally irreconcilable visions of society. While we are certainly not a nation at war with Islam, we are a nation that faces a huge challenge from the Islamic world—a challenge that includes terrorism but also a much larger civilizational ambition that remains central. Anyone standing in Istanbul, the historic seat of Ottoman power, should recognize that fact.

As a believer in the Lord Jesus Christ and a minister of the Gospel, my primary concern about Islam is not civilizational or geopolitical, but theological. I believe that Jesus Christ is indeed "the way, and the truth, and the life," and that no one comes to the Father but by Him (John 14:6). Salvation is found only through faith in the Lord Jesus Christ, and the gospel of Christ is the only message that saves.

I can agree with President Obama that Islam has produced cultural wonders, but I have to see it more fundamentally as a belief system that is taking millions upon millions of persons spiritually captive—leaving them under the curse of sin and without hope of salvation.

For Christians, regardless of nationality, this is the great challenge that should be our urgent concern. Our concern is not mainly political, but theological and spiritual. And, all things considered, Islam almost surely represents the greatest challenge to Christian evangelism of our times.

21

THE NEW ATHEISM

Darwinism Makes
Disbelief "Work"

The New Atheism is now an established feature of our intellectual landscape. Thinkers such as Richard Dawkins, Daniel Dennett, Christopher Hitchens, and Sam Harris are among the figures who most regularly appear on the front tables of America's bookstores and the front pages of our newspapers. And, along with their vigorous defense of atheism, we most often find an equally vigorous defense of evolutionary theory. This is no accident.

Atheism has appeared in some form in Western cultures since the midpoint of the last millennium. The word *atheist* did not even exist within the English language until the reign of Queen Elizabeth I. The earliest atheists were most often philosophical and theological skeptics who denied the existence of any personal God. Nevertheless, the God they almost always rejected is the God of the Bible; in other words, this was a specific rejection of Christianity.

The early atheists were usually notorious, as were well-known heretics. Their denials of God and the Christian faith were well documented and understood. But the early atheists had a huge problem—how could they explain the existence of the cosmos? Without a clear answer to that question, their arguments for atheism failed to gain much traction.

As even the ancient Greeks understood, one of the most fundamental philosophical questions is this: why is there something rather than nothing? Every worldview is accountable to that question. In other words, every philosophy of life must offer some account of how we and the world around us came to be. The creation myths of ancient cultures and the philosophical speculations of the Greeks serve as evidence of the hunger in the human intellect. We now call that hunger the question of origins.

For some time, atheists were hard-pressed to offer any coherent answer to that question. Once they ruled God out of the picture, they had virtually no account of creation to offer.

Of course, all that changed with Charles Darwin.

Darwin's theory of natural selection and the larger theory of evolution emerged in the nineteenth century as the first coherent alternative to the Bible's doctrine of creation. This revolution in human thinking is well summarized in *The Blind Watchmaker* by Richard Dawkins, who conceded that an atheist prior to Darwin would have to offer an explanation of the cosmos and the existence of life that would look something like this: "I have no explanation for complex biological design. All I know is that God isn't a good explanation, so we must wait and hope that somebody comes up with a better one."

Dawkins, who is perhaps the world's best-known evolutionary scientist, argues that the explanation offered by a frustrated atheist before Darwin "would have left one feeling pretty unsatisfied."

But then came Darwin. In a single sentence, Dawkins gets to the heart of the matter: "Darwin made it possible to be an intellectually fulfilled atheist."

His point is clear and compelling. Prior to the development of the theory of evolution, there was no way for an atheist to settle on a clear argument for why the cosmos exists or why life forms appeared. Darwin changed all that. The development of Darwinian evolution offered atheism an invaluable intellectual tool—an account of beginnings.

The New Atheists have emerged as potent public voices. They write best-selling books, appear on major college and university campuses, and extend their voices through institutional and cultural influence. The movement is new in the sense that it differs from the older atheism in several respects. One of these differences is the use of science in general, and evolutionary theory in particular, as intellectual leverage against belief in God.

Dawkins, for example, not only believes that Darwinism made it possible to be an intellectually fulfilled atheist, but he also argues that religious belief is actually dangerous and devoid of credibility. So, he argues that the theory of evolution undermines belief in God. In other words, Dawkins asserts that Darwinism makes it impossible to be an intellectually fulfilled Christian.

Daniel Dennett, another of the Four Horsemen of the New Atheism, has argued that Darwin's theory of evolution is a "universal acid" that will burn away all claims of the existence of God. His confidence in Darwinism is total. He looks back longingly at his own childhood belief in a divinely created world and argues that eventually his experience of moving from belief in creation to confidence in evolution will be shared by a humanity that grows into intellectual adulthood.

Dennett is honest enough to recognize that if evolutionary theory is true, it must eventually offer an account of everything related to the question of life. Thus, evolution will have to explain every aspect of life, from how a species appeared to why a mother loves her child.

Interestingly, Dennett offers an argument for why humans have believed in the existence of God. As we might expect, the theory of evolution is used to explain that there must have been a time when belief in God was necessary for humans to have adequate confidence to reproduce. Clearly,

Dennett believes that we should now have adequate confidence to reproduce without belief in God.

Sam Harris, also a scientist by training, is another ardent defender of evolutionary theory. Pushing the argument even further than Dawkins and Dennett, Harris argues that belief in God is such a danger to human civilization that religious liberty should be denied in order that science might reign supreme as the intellectual foundation of human society.

Author Christopher Hitchens, the last of the Four Horsemen, uses his considerable wit to ridicule belief in God, which he, like Dawkins and Harris, considers downright dangerous to humanity. Though Hitchens is not a scientist, his atheism leaves no room for any theory other than evolution.

The dogma of Darwinism is among the first principles of the worldview offered by the New Atheists. Darwin replaces the Bible as the great explainer of the existence of life in all of its forms. The New Atheists are not merely dependent upon science for their worldview; their worldview amounts to scientism—the belief that modern naturalistic science is the great unifying answer to the most basic questions of human life.

As Richard Dawkins has recently argued, New Atheists believe that disbelief in evolution should be considered as intellectually disrespectable and reprehensible as denial of the Holocaust. Thus, their strategy is to use the theory of evolution as a central weapon in today's context of intellectual combat.

The New Atheists would have no coherent worldview without the dogma of Darwinism. With it, they intend to malign belief in God and to marginalize Christians and Christian arguments. Thus, we can draw a straight line from the emergence of evolutionary theory to the resurgence of atheism in our times. Never underestimate the power of a bad idea.

22

A BLACK CAT IN A DARK ROOM

Are Theologians Really Saying Anything?

Terry Sanderson is president of Britain's National Secular Society, so it is hardly news that he has little time for the efforts of theologians. Writing in London's *Guardian,* Sanderson dismisses theology as a form of knowledge.[1] Theologians may talk, he suggests, but they are really not saying anything.

In his words, "theology is drivel." Thus, any attention given to theology—even to refute it—is just wasted effort.

---

1. Terry Sanderson, "Theology—Truly a Naked Emperor," *The Guardian,* May 26, 2010, www.guardian.co.uk/commentisfree/belief/2010/may/26/theology-atheism.

Efforts to understand theology are hopeless, he insists. In order to bolster his claim, Sanderson cites the late science-fiction writer Robert A. Heinlein, who wrote, "Theology…is searching in a dark cellar at midnight for a black cat that isn't there. Theologians can persuade themselves of anything."

Sanderson also calls H. L. Mencken to testify: "For centuries, theologians have been explaining the unknowable in terms of the-not-worth-knowing."

Well, at least he doesn't equivocate. Heinlein and Mencken had their say, and to their assessments of theology Sanderson adds his own: "Theology is an excuse for grown men to spend their lives trying to convince themselves, and others, that ridiculous fairy tales are true."

Sanderson doesn't even believe in the so-called big questions about life and its meaning. "My problem is these questions don't have an answer," he asserts, "no matter how long you think about them and however much you try to bring God into the equation." Sanderson prefers Gertrude Stein's succinct worldview: there is no answer.

And yet for someone who says theology is not worth reading, he seems to have at least made some effort to read the works of Rowan Williams, who was an academic theologian before becoming the Archbishop of Canterbury. Sanderson goes so far as to cite a rather lengthy paragraph from one of Williams's sermons. Williams, he concedes, is thought to be intelligent. "He is said to have a brain the size of Jupiter because he can produce convoluted writing that nobody with their feet in reality can comprehend."

Williams, whose tepid leadership of the Anglican Communion and refusal to call to account liberal churches in the United States and Canada has brought his communion to the point of breakup, is quite capable of writing incomprehensible prose. That skill is shared by far too many academics in every field. But Sanderson's central point is not that this particular theologian is incomprehensible but that theology itself is incomprehensible, and that is a very different matter.

Theology is worse than useless, he complains, because it contains no knowledge. He compares theology to modern science: "If science disappeared from human memory, we would soon be living in caves again. If theology disappeared from human memory, no one would notice."

Now, a careful thinker might quickly point out the illogical and absurd argument Sanderson makes here. By simple logical fact, no one notices what one has forgotten— otherwise one has not forgotten. But Sanderson's main point is clear enough.

On the one hand, what makes Terry Sanderson's argument so untenable is the fact that one cannot explain human history in general, and the history of Western civilization in particular, without endless reference to the fact that human beings have indeed believed in God and that these beliefs did and do matter. Like it or not, one cannot explain our culture and civilization without constant reference to theology.

But Sanderson's larger point is more serious and important. He is truly certain that theology has no claim upon knowledge. In other words, theologians are not talking about any reality. Theology is just a mind game played by individual theologians or theological communities.

Oddly enough, Sanderson's argument is championed by some within the theological academy. A good many radical and revisionist theologians openly accept Sanderson's claims. They, too, argue that theology offers no knowledge, only potential meaning. Their God is not a self-revealing, self-existent person, but a symbol or a literary character.

Feminist theologian Janet Martin Soskice describes theological realists as "those who, while aware of the inability of any theological formulation to catch the divine realities, none the less accept that there *are* divine realities that theologians, however ham-fistedly, are trying to catch."[2] In other words, she is explaining to her readers that when some theologians speak of God, they really believe that there *is* a God of whom they are speaking.

It says a great deal about the state of academic theology

---

2. J. M. Soskice, "Theological Realism," in *The Rationality of Religious Belief,* ed. W. J. Abraham and S. W. Holtzer (Oxford: Clarendon Press, 1987), 108.

today that Soskice had to explain that some theologians really believe there is a God and that we can truly know him.

Far too many academic theologians are in basic agreement with Terry Sanderson, but they take their paychecks and attend their academic meetings anyway. For them, theology is just one more discipline in the theory-laden world of the modern academy.

But if theologians are not making a claim to knowledge—if theology is just looking for a nonexistent black cat in a dark room—then shut it all down and spend the money on something useful.

Authentic Christian theology begins and ends with the knowledge of God, a true knowledge that God has graciously revealed to us in His Word. Without the gift of God's self-revelation, we would be groping in that dark room for a black cat. However, the fact that God has revealed Himself changes everything.

The true and living God desires to be known and has made Himself known. That makes all the difference. True theology is not explaining the unknowable, but coming to know the God who wants us to know Him. Theology *is* about knowledge, indeed, about the knowledge that matters most of all.

Don't worry about the black cat in the dark room. Our task is to know, serve, and worship the God who is there and who has made Himself known.

23

THE NEW AMERICAN FAMILY

Digitally Deluged

The Campbell family of California just might be the prototypical American family of the future. Kord Campbell and his wife, Brenda, recently moved to the San Francisco area from Oklahoma, along with their two children, Lily, age eight, and Connor, age sixteen. They also came with plenty of digital technology—and they have acquired more.

The family is profiled by Matt Richtel in an article in the *New York Times*.[1] As Richtel explains, the Campbells might not be just any other family in the neighborhood

---

1. Matt Richtel, "Hooked on Gadgets and Paying a Price," *The New York Times*, June 7, 2010, www.nytimes.com/2010/06/07/technology/07 brain.html.

with respect to their digital habits. Then again, they might be, after all. At the very least, they probably point to a new family reality that will become all the more common.

Kord Campbell moved to California to start a software venture. And yet, his life is so filled with e-mails, text messages, chats, Web pages, and video games that he missed a crucial e-mail from a company wanting to buy his Internet startup—for twelve days. In Richtel's words, Campbell is struggling with a "deluge of data." More alarming than that, his family is drowning in the deluge as well.

As Richtel reports: "Even after he unplugs, he craves the stimulation he gets from his electronic gadgets. He forgets things like dinner plans, and he has trouble focusing on his family."

"This is your brain on computers," Richtel asserts.

Scientists are beginning to document the effects of digital exposure on the brain. They are finding that everything from phone calls (remember those?) to e-mail and text messages exact a toll on the brain's ability to concentrate and focus. Furthermore, they have identified a physiological reward for digital stimulation—a "dopamine squirt." That little squirt of dopamine in the brain serves as a physiological payoff for digital stimulation, and it can be habit-forming.

It is for Kord Campbell. This husband and father admits to being often unable to focus on his wife and children and their family life. He goes to sleep with a laptop or similar device on his chest. When he awakens, he goes directly online, where he remains throughout the day. During family time, he often retreats into his digital world. He has left family outings to play video games and check his digital gadgets. Brenda laments, "It seems like he can no longer be fully in the moment." When he tries to unplug, he becomes "crotchety until he gets his fix."

And yet, rather than attempt a move out of such digital dependence, Mr. Campbell seems to be drawing his family members into the digital net. Brenda checks e-mail about twenty-five times a day, sends and receives text messages, and is getting more involved on Facebook. Connor is becoming so involved in the digital world that his grades are slipping. Lily has only one hour of unstructured time each day, and she often devotes that hour to digital devices. Connor apparently has a computer with Internet access in his bedroom, along with his iPhone. When he studies, an inner voice seems to call out to him to switch over to a digital distraction.

The Campbells may be atypical in the extent of their digital entanglements, but new research indicates that they are probably not as atypical as we would hope. Richtel reports that Americans in 2008 consumed three times more daily information than in 1960. Those who use computers at work change windows or screens an average of thirty-seven times an hour.

The change in human experience is so vast that Adam

Gazzaley of the University of California, San Francisco, names it one of the most significant shifts ever experienced in the history of humanity—and one with inevitable consequences.

What about multitasking? Many people claim that exposure to digital technologies prompts the development of a new mental skill, managing multiple mental tasks. As it turns out, multitasking seems to be more of an illusion than a reality. Richtel reports that brain researcher Eyal Ophir of Stanford University has found that multitasking actually takes quite a toll on the brain's ability to concentrate on anything. Furthermore, research also suggests that multitaskers have a very difficult time turning that mode of thinking off—a fact that goes a long way toward explaining why some people cannot handle real-life face-to-face conversations.

In an accompanying article in the *New York Times*, Tara Parker-Pope asks a chilling but revealing question: "Has high-speed Internet made you impatient with slow-speed children?"[2] Does that question not arrest you on the spot?

The research indicates that people who are highly invested in digital involvements are less empathetic, less atten-

---

2. Tara Parker-Pope, "An Ugly Toll of Technology: Impatience and Forgetfulness," *The New York Times*, June 6, 2010, www.nytimes.com/2010/06/07/technology/07brainside.html.

tive, less patient, and less able to remember something as basic as a conversation.

Just imagine what all this means. While the average American is likely to express some measure of concern in light of this research, and while most families no doubt seek a life different than that described of the Campbells, Christians have to look at this picture with a very different and far deeper set of concerns.

Is that what we were created to be? Is this the purpose for which God created humanity? The Creator made us in his image, and thus to be relational beings. But this relationality is intended to be expressed first and foremost in relationships with human beings, and certainly not with machines. A biblical understanding also presses us to identify the relationships of our greatest accountability—the relationships of marriage, family, kinship, and congregation—as well as the relationships of greatest gospel opportunity. When these relationships suffer due to digital distractions, we bear full moral responsibility.

The answer is not to throw away all the digital gadgets. The information revolution is here to stay, and it comes with great gifts as well as tremendous temptations. Christians are not called to be modern-day Luddites, smashing digital devices with sledgehammers. But we are called to be faithful stewards of digital opportunities, even as we are also called to be faithful in all our relationships. That second stewardship is surely of greater importance than the first.

This stewardship will require clear boundaries, honest self-knowledge, and authentic accountability. Otherwise, you may well end up spending more time with your digital devices than with the people you love. Count on this: they will notice.

24

WHERE DID I COME FROM?

The New World of Reproductive Technology

At some point, anticipated and even feared by some parents, every child asks the inevitable question, "Where did I come from?" That question is endemic to humanity. The question of our own biological origins is eventually inescapable. Our existence requires an explanation, and the question takes bold form. The answer used to be easy.

That is, the answer was easy in terms of biology. In some form, the answer took the shape of a story about two people, one male and one female, who came together and made a baby. Mommy and Daddy made a baby. That story was both true and universal. For most of human history, there was no alternative account. The answer given by parents in 1960 was the same as that given in 1060 or in any previous year.

All that changed with the biological revolution and the emergence of new reproductive technologies. The development of in vitro fertilization (IVF) technologies came only after human beings grew accustomed to reproductive control through the pill. If medical technologies could be harnessed to avoid pregnancy, surely new technologies could allow couples to have long-wanted children who had not come by natural means.

The public was assured that the use of these new technologies would not bring about a moral revolution, since the availability would be limited to married couples. But, of course, this was a false promise, and it should have been seen as such from the start. The pill was at first prescribed only for married couples, but the plain fact is that a far greater demand for contraceptives existed among the unmarried. By the early 1970s, the pill was available to all.

The same story applied to the use of IVF. If there were thousands of potential users among married couples, these were vastly outnumbered by unmarried persons and non-heterosexual couples. Through the development of IVF and the revolutions made possible by egg and sperm donation and surrogate motherhood, parenthood, though redefined, was now available to virtually any adult and any couple.

This revolution is movingly portrayed in a *New York*

Times Magazine cover story.[1] In "Meet the Twiblings," Melanie Thernstrom provides an account of how she and her husband became parents to babies Violet and Kieran, who appear endearingly on the cover. The cover text also contains this teaser: "How Four Women (and One Man) Conspired to Make Two Babies."

As Thernstrom acknowledges, this is a complicated story. The two babies were born five days apart. They shared a common egg donor (obtained commercially) and a common sperm donor (Thernstrom's husband, Michael). But they were carried by two different surrogate mothers. Genetically they are siblings, but they emerged from two different wombs. They were born five days apart, but they are not really twins. Thernstrom calls them twiblings.

She writes movingly of her efforts, with Michael, to have a child. After six IVF rounds and clear medical advice, the Thernstroms moved to develop a new plan, but the plan required a great deal of thinking. The pull of the new reproductive technologies was clear, as was the revolution these technologies represent. She writes, "Reproductive technology fills an important—and growing—need. Gay couples are increasingly choosing to have families. Eight percent of women between 40 and 44 identify themselves

---

1. Melanie Thernstrom, "Meet the Twiblings," *The New York Times Magazine,* December 29, 2010, www.nytimes.com/2011/01/02/magazine/02 babymaking-t.html.

as involuntarily childless or hoping to become pregnant, according to a Pew report. Most women in that age bracket will be able to become pregnant only by using donor eggs."

Melanie and Michael wanted siblings of about the same age to grow up as companions. IVF twins were more dangerous, so Michael came up with the idea of using two surrogates to deliver two babies at about the same time.

Thernstrom's account of the complexities of the decision-making process is fascinating, but what many readers may miss is the basic fact that these decisions were absolutely unknown to previous generations of humanity. Would they choose an egg donor who looked like Melanie? The Thernstrom's were more interested in personality attributes, even if these are hard to define in genetic terms. They eventually chose a donor with a "delightful" personality.

They also chose the surrogate mothers with care. Melanie noted that moral concerns about surrogacy came from both liberals and conservatives, if on different grounds. She chose two women who, made pregnant with the embryos created by the donor eggs and Michael's sperm, carried the Thernstrom's reproductive hopes as well.

Melanie and Michael referred to these babies as "drafts." In her words, they did this "to remind ourselves that they were notes toward the children we wanted, but if they died, they were just beginnings like all the embryos had been, and we would start again."

Kieran was born first, with Violet arriving five days later.

Both are adorable and healthy. The roles of the surrogate mothers did not end with the births, however, for the Thernstroms—against the prevailing advice—chose to maintain a relationship with the surrogates and the egg donor.

Interestingly, Melanie Thernstrom seems to see the complexity of these births as somewhat advantageous. "I wanted to avoid what I think of as the claustrophobia of the nuclear family," she explains. She refers to the web of relationships required by this process as "a kind of extended family."

She also acknowledges the ambiguities created by these new technologies. "Third-party reproduction creates all kinds of relationships for which there are not yet terms," she writes. "For example, there is no word to describe the relationship between our children and the carriers' children, but it feels to me that they are, somehow, related. They are gestational siblings; they don't share a mother, father or genes, but they were carried in the same body and they learned its fathomless chemical language." Furthermore,

> There is also no word to describe our children's
> relationship with each other. Our children were
> born five days apart—a fact that cannot be easily
> explained. When people press me about their status
> ("But are they really twins?"), the answer gets long.
> The word "twins" usually refers to siblings who
> shared a womb. But to call them just "siblings"

instead of "twins" also raises questions because full genetic siblings are ordinarily at least nine months apart. And our children could be considered the same age because they were conceived at the same time (in the lab) and the embryos were transferred at the same time. If the person continues to quibble about whether they really qualify as twins (as, surprisingly, people often do), instead of asking why it matters, I announce airily that they are "twiblings."

Barely a week before the Thernstrom story appeared in print, pop icon Elton John and his partner, David Furnish, "had" a baby boy. London's *Guardian* explained that the baby came "with the help of an anonymous Californian surrogate and a separate egg donor." The birth of the baby boy, named Zachary Jackson Levon Furnish-John, created something of a stir in the British press, but the main issue of concern seemed to be the fact that at the time of the birth, Elton John was sixty-two and David Furnish was forty-eight. The issue of homosexuality was so politically incorrect that age appeared to be the only factor of interest. Zoe Williams of *The Guardian* went so far as to proclaim that the whole event added up to the fact that "homophobia is dying."[2]

---

2. Zoe Williams, "Rejoice at Elton's News. And that Homophobia Is Dying," *The Guardian,* December 30, 2010, www.guardian.co.uk/commentisfree/2010/dec/30/elton-john-homophobia-baby-lifestyle.

It's as if we are now living on a new planet—one in which all the natural boundaries of sex and reproduction have been left behind. The technologies of reproduction are redefining sex, marriage, relationships, family, and the human story. Humanity is rushing headlong into a world in which the answer to the question "Where did I come from?" can be endlessly complicated. We have no adequate categories for explaining the relationship of little Kieran and Violet and all those who "conspired" to bring them to be. We read the birth announcement of Zachary Jackson Levon Furnish-John and know that the most important moral questions are already culturally off-limits.

An entire industry now operates with a global reach, offering these reproductive technologies to virtually anyone with the cash to pay. And we can count on reproductive technologies expanding as a growth industry.

The theological and moral implications are endless and urgent, but the technologies rush ahead. For Christians, the most urgent issue is the total separation of natural reproduction in the context of marriage from the process of reproduction that is made possible by these technologies. The moral complexities surrounding Kieran and Violet Thernstrom and their "extended family" are vexing. We naturally sympathize with a married couple who so desperately desire a child, but the discussion of the life choices that lead many couples to desire children at an advanced age rather than earlier is also off-limits.

And the birth of Zachary Jackson Levon Furnish-John to an aging pop singer and his same-sex partner is just a sign of things to come. The question "Where did I come from?" may well emerge as one of the most haunting questions of our times.

25

REDEFINING RETIREMENT

For the Good of the Kingdom

The concept of retirement is rather recent in origins. Most historians trace the concept back to Germany's "Iron Chancellor," Otto von Bismarck, who pushed through a series of social changes in the late nineteenth century. Among those changes was a system something like Social Security, intended as a guaranteed pension for the elderly.

Bismarck's idea was that workers in Germany would need to give way so that younger men would be able to enter the workforce and support their families. The concept of retirement from the workforce took root, and by the mid-point of the twentieth century, most American workers expected to retire at close to age sixty-five.

The contemporary ideal of retirement was a life of travel, leisure, golf, and time with grandchildren. In states like Florida, California, and Arizona, entire communities of retirees emerged. "Leisurevilles" advertised a concept of the good life that was free from employment and largely, if not exclusively, devoted to withdrawal from the world of all work.

These communities are now in trouble. The concept of retirement is now changing, brought about by the economic recession that has propelled many older Americans back into the workforce. As Laura Vanderkam reports in *USA Today*, "After decades of decline, the labor force participation rate among people older than 65 rose from a low of 10.7% in 1987 to more than 17% now. Nearly a third of those ages 65–69 are working or looking for work, up from less than 20% in the 1980s, and surveys of Baby Boomers find that many don't intend to retire immediately either."[1]

We will likely look back on the period between 1950 and 2000 as the era of retirement. When President Franklin D. Roosevelt signed Social Security into law, the expectation was that workers would probably live an average of five to eight years after retirement. But the extension of the human life span during the last half of the twentieth century meant

---

1. Laura Vanderkam, "This Isn't Grandpa's Retirement," *USA Today*, January 4, 2011, www.usatoday.com/news/opinion/forum/2011-01-05-column05_ST_N.htm.

that retirement could easily last for twenty years, and often even longer. Now, those who live to age sixty-five, Vanderkam reports, "can quite reasonably expect to live to age 85 or more."

Here is the key sentence in Vanderkam's essay: "The notion that work is something you want to stop doing is getting a makeover as well." It's about time.

The Bible dignifies both labor and age, but the modern American ideal of retirement is nowhere to be found in the Scriptures. Instead, lives of useful service to the kingdom of Christ are the expectation, all the way to the grave.

The economic crisis of recent years has forced many Americans to rethink and redefine retirement as a matter of necessity. For Christians, this represents an important opportunity. The ideal for Christians should be redeployment, even after employment. There is so much kingdom work to be done, and older believers are desperately needed in this great task. There are missionaries to be assisted, ministries to be energized, young couples to be counseled, boys without fathers to be mentored, and wisdom and experience to be shared. The possibilities for Christian redeployment are endless.

There is room in the Christian life for leisure—but not for a life devoted to leisure. As long as we have the strength and ability to serve, we are workers needed in Christ's kingdom. Given the needs and priorities all around us, who would settle for life in Leisureville?

DANGEROUS BELIEFS IN THE NEW SPIRITUAL OPENNESS

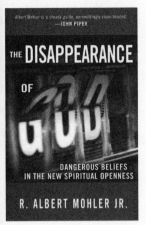

For centuries the church has taught and guarded the core Christian beliefs that make up the essential foundations of the faith. But in our postmodern age, sloppy teaching and outright lies create rampant confusion, and many Christians are free-falling for "feel-good" theology.

Albert Mohler provides a steady guide to the truth, off-setting the errors that could derail our faith.

ARE YOU READY TO RESPOND TO THE MOST RELEVANT QUESTIONS OF SEXUALITY TODAY?

We are reminded every day that assumptions about what is right and wrong, sexually, are different today than they were fifty—or even ten—years ago. Christian principles that formed the pattern for generations of American families are conspicuously absent. What happened and why? How do we respond to the dramatic shift in our culture's perspective on sex? Dr. Albert Mohler addresses these critical topics in a thoughtful, cut-to-the-chase style in *Desire and Deceit*.

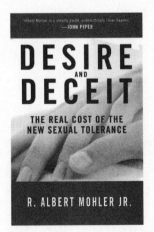